HC

Phil Dampier has been a journalist for more than 30 years. For a decade, he worked for *The Sun*, first as west-country correspondent and then as royal reporter. As a freelance writer for the last 18 years his articles, mainly about the royal family, have been published in newspapers and magazines worldwide. He now also works as a PR consultant and advised Wycombe Wanderers FC during the 2005–06 season.

As a boy he fell in love with football, playing the sport for his school and in the park, and watching England win the 1966 World Cup. A lifelong Chelsea fan, he is a season ticket holder at Stamford Bridge.

He lives in Kent with his partner Ann and beloved dog Jess.

Ashley Walton has been a journalist all his working life. He began as a tea boy on a Midlands evening newspaper, working his way up from covering rabbit shows to front page crime reporting. He arrived in Fleet Street at the *Daily Express* in the early 1970s, and spent 25 years there becoming crime correspondent and royal reporter. He ended his career working on the foreign and news desks.

Ashley was brought up in the shadow of Coventry City's Highfield Road stadium, and his family home was so close to the ground that the windows rattled every time the Sky Blues scored.

He lives in Hertfordshire with his wife Joan and sons Nic and Oliver.

By the same authors:

Duke of Hazard – The Wit and Wisdom of Prince Philip, The Book Guild, 2006

What's in the Queen's Handbag (and Other Royal Secrets), The Book Guild, 2007

The Wit and Wisdom of British Prime Ministers, The Book Guild, 2008

GAFFERS – THE WIT AND WISDOM OF FOOTBALL MANAGERS

Phil Dampier and
Ashley Walton

Book Guild Publishing
Sussex, England

First published in Great Britain in 2009 by
The Book Guild Ltd
Pavilion View
19 New Road
Brighton, BN1 1UF

Typesetting in Garamond by
Keyboard Services, Luton, Bedfordshire

Printed in Great Britain by
CPI Antony Rowe

A catalogue record for this book is available from
The British Library

ISBN 978 1 84624 399 8

CONTENTS

Malcolm Allison	1
Ron Atkinson	4
Craig Brown	14
Sir Matt Busby	16
Jack Charlton	20
Brian Clough	23
Kenny Dalglish	33
Tommy Docherty	36
Sir Alex Ferguson	40
Sven-Goran Eriksson	50
George Graham	53
Ron Greenwood	55
Ruud Gullit	57
Glenn Hoddle	62
Ian Holloway	66
Kevin Keegan	71

Howard Kendall	81
Steve McClaren	83
José Mourinho	85
Bill Nicholson	91
Martin O'Neill	93
Bob Paisley	96
David Pleat	99
Sir Alf Ramsey	102
Claudio Ranieri	107
Harry Redknapp	109
Don Revie	114
Sir Bobby Robson	116
Joe Royle	126
Luiz Felipe Scolari	128
Bill Shankly	130
John 'Jock' Stein	139
Gordon Strachan	142
Graham Taylor	147
Terry Venables	152
Arsene Wenger	157
Miscellaneous Managers	162

ACKNOWLEDGEMENTS

The authors would like to thank Paul White for suggesting the idea for this book.

PREFACE

They are among the most famous and oft-quoted members of our modern-day celebrity culture.

Every week we hang on the words of the football managers, masters of the mixed metaphors, own-goal gaffes and occasional pearls of wisdom. They are highly-paid, highly-strung and, with a few notable exceptions, have less job security than in virtually any other profession. But we, and they, wouldn't have it any other way.

Football, the 'beautiful game' according to Pelé, is the world's most popular sport because it is so simple. But that doesn't stop our macho motivators from making it more complicated with their post-match comments, biased biographies and philosophical mutterings.

This comprehensive collection of hilarious one-liners and sometimes poignant reflections has it all:

The earthy observations of Liverpool legend Bill Shankly and the contemporary, stylish outpourings of Portugal's José Mourinho.

Ron Atkinson's 'Ron-glish' and Glenn Hoddle's born-again gibberish.

Kevin Keegan's sanguine sayings and Sir Bobby Robson's classic confusions.

Whether you are a loyal supporter, an armchair fan

or not even interested in soccer, you won't be able to stop laughing at *Gaffers – The Wit and Wisdom of Football Managers.*

MALCOLM ALLISON

Born: 1927

'A lot of hard work went into this defeat.'

'John Bond has blackened my name with his insinuations about the private lives of football managers. Both my wives are upset.'

'You're not a real manager unless you have been sacked.'

On Ron Atkinson: 'They call him Big Ron because he is a big spender in the transfer market. I just call him Fat Ron.'

'Size does matter in football. You judge a defender by the size of his tackle.'

At Manchester City: 'Before we won the Championship, I told the lads exactly how many goals we would score and how many points. I was exactly right – I'm brilliant!'

Big Mal introduces himself to Francis Lee in 1967: 'You're not a good player. In fact, you're a bad player, but I could make you into a fair player.'

Attempting to put off other managers watching a young Colin Bell play for Bury, so that he could buy him: 'He can't head it! He can't pass it! He's no good on his left foot!'

Head waiter: 'Mr Allison, your bar bill – I have to tell you it is enormous.'
Allison: 'Is that all? You insult me. Don't come back until it's double that!'

'A lot of people in football don't have much time for the press – they say they're amateurs.'

'This game is like being in love. You've got to suffer to enjoy it.'

Appealing against a touchline ban while manager of Plymouth Argyle in 1978: 'It's ridiculous. I've served more time than Ronnie Biggs did for the Great Train Robbery.'

RON ATKINSON

Born: 1939

'I wanted to give my players some technical advice, so I told them the game had started.'

'He dribbles a lot and the opposition don't like it – you can see it all over their faces.'

'The defender is very deceptive. He must be lightning slow.'

'On another night they'd have won that 2–2.'

'If Glenn Hoddle said one word to his team at half-time, it was concentration and focus.'

'A ten-foot keeper really should have stopped that.'

'There's a little triangle – five left-footed players.'

'I tell you what, if the Cameroons get a goal back here they're literally gonna catch on fire.'

'It's all about the two "Ms" – movement and positioning.'

RON ATKINSON

'Beckenbauer has really gambled all his eggs.'

'Peter Schmeichel extends and grows even bigger than he is.'

'They are doing the old-fashioned things well, they've kicked the ball, they've headed it.'

'He sliced the ball when he had it on a plate.'

'I'm afraid they've left their legs at home.'

'The midfield are outnumbered numerically.'

'I never criticise referees and I'm not going to change a habit for that prat.'

'That was Pelé's strength, holding people off with his arm.'

'They've picked their heads up off the ground, and now they have a lot to carry on their shoulders.'

On taking over as Manchester United manager in 1981: 'You're welcome to my home phone number, gentlemen – but please remember not to ring me during *The Sweeney*!'

After being sacked by Manchester United in 1987:

'I've had to swap my Merc for a BMW, I'm down to my last thirty-seven suits and I'm drinking non-vintage champagne.'

'I'll never be able to achieve what Tommy Docherty did and take Aston Villa into the third division and Manchester United into the second division.'

'Well, either side could win it, or it could be a draw.'

'There's a snap about Liverpool that just isn't there.'

'My favourite politician was Margaret Thatcher. She was a bugger but she would have made the best football manager. John Major was all right – he just had a bad team.'

'Going to Anfield was like being in Vietnam.'

'Germany, not for the first time this century, invading Czech territory.'

'You half fancied that to go in as it was rising and dipping at the same time.'

'Moreno thought that the fullback was going to come up behind and give him one really hard.'

'Every time Zidane comes inside him, Roberto Carlos just goes bonking down the wing.'

On England midfielder Ray Wilkins, known as 'The Crab': 'He can't run, can't tackle and can't head the ball. The only time he goes forward is to toss the coin.'

'Women should be in the kitchen, the disco and the boutique, but not in football.'

'There's nobody fitter at his age except maybe Raquel Welch.'

As Steve McManaman hoisted the 2002 Champions League trophy for Real Madrid: 'You won't see that again now that the Scouser's got his hands on it.'

'They must go for it now as they have nothing to lose but the match.'

'I think the referee should be allowed to blow up now, as a mercy killing if you like.'

'I would not say that David Ginola is one of the best left-wingers in the Premiership, but there are none better.'

'They've come out at half-time and gone bang.'

'We were a little bit outnumbered there. It was two against two.'

'Phil Neville was treading on dangerous water there.'

'I've had this sneaking feeling throughout the game that it's there to be won.'

During the 1990 World Cup finals: 'I've just seen Gary Lineker shake hands with Jurgen Klinsmann. It's a wonder Klinsmann hasn't fallen down.'

'I would also think that the replay showed it to be worse than it actually was.'

Trying to get more out of born-again Christian Cyrille Regis: 'I know Cyrille's found God, but now I want him to find the Devil.'

After a violent Manchester United v Valencia clash in1982: 'It's the first time after a match that we've had to replace divots in the players.'

'I see Atletico Madrid just sacked another manager before the season has even started. He must have had a bad photo-call!'

'I think that was a moment of cool panic there.'

'Woodcock would have scored, but his shot was too perfect.'

'Someone in the England team will have to grab the ball by the horns.'

'I met Mick Jagger when I was playing for Oxford United and the Rolling Stones played a concert there. Little did I know that one day he'd be almost as famous as me.'

'He's not only a good player but he's spiteful – in the nicest sense of the word.'

'Tony Adams – he's the rock that the team has grown from.'

'Chelsea look like they've got a couple more gears left in the locker.'

'He should get his head to those. He is twelve feet tall.'

'The keeper should have saved that one, but he did.'

'There's lots of balls dropping off people.'

'Now Manchester United are 2–1 down on aggregate, they are in a better position than when they started the game at 1–1.'

'Zero-zero is a big score.'

'Stoichkov's playing on the wing. In this situation he likes to come in and scalp the centre half.'

'If you score against the Italians you deserve a goal.'

'There's a few tired limbs in the blue legs.'

'Ryan Giggs is running long up the back-side.'

'Our fans have been branded with the same brush.'

'His white boots were on fire against Arsenal and he'll be looking for them to reproduce.'

'He'll take some pleasure from that, will Brian Carey. He and Steve Bull have been having it off all afternoon.'

'When Scholes gets it wrong [tackling] they come in so late that they arrive yesterday.'

'This is the best Man United have played in Europe this season, and conversely, the opposition have been excellent.'

'Scholes and Van Nistelrooy drugged the last two defenders.'

'The ball goes down the keeper's throat where it hits him on the knees, to say the least.'

'You don't want to be giving away free kicks in the penalty area.'

'Think of a number between ten and eleven.'

'Their forward got a lucky squeeze from the defender.'

'I'm sure Bobby won't want them to be losing the match before winning it.'

After his Nottingham Forest side had lost 8–1 to Manchester United: 'We gave the fans a nine goal thriller!'

On Italian player Francesco Totti: 'He actually looks a little twat, that Totti. I can't see what all the fuss is about.'

'Chinese women are the unprettiest in the world.'

'They've certainly grown, the Japanese. I mean grown in stature, playing-wise.'

'Argentina are the second-best team in the world, and there's no higher praise than that.'

'Their strength is their strength.'

'We haven't had a strategic free kick all night. No one's knocked over attackers ad lib.'

On the 1994 World Cup: 'What was my highlight of the tournament? Bumping into Frank Sinatra.'

On Aston Villa player Dennis Jackson: 'He invented the banana shot. Trouble was, he was trying to shoot straight.'

'You can see the ball go past them, or the man, but you'll never see both man and ball go past at the same time. So if the ball goes past, the man won't, or if the man goes past they'll take the ball.'

'Van Nistelrooy, predating as usual.'

'His head just disappeared into his shoulders.'

'They scored too early.'

'Lee Dixon will be up against two South American left-handers tonight.'

'Carlton Palmer can trap the ball further than I can kick it.'

'It's bloody tough being a legend.'

CRAIG BROWN

Born: 1940

'They had a dozen corners, maybe twelve – I'm guessing.'

'I strongly feel that the only difference between the two teams were the goals that England scored.'

'The underdogs will start favourites for this match.'

'Our keeper only had one save to make, but we lost 4–0.'

'Michael Owen, he's got the legs of a salmon.'

'It is fashionable for expectant fathers to be with their wives at the birth.'

'We had two shots saved off the line by the post.'

While Scotland manager before a 1999 Euro 2000 play-off with England: 'Kevin Keegan and I have sixty-three international caps between us. He has sixty-three of them.'

'My job is my holiday. I travel all the time and see the world in this business. I take my holidays at home in Ayr.'

'My brother Bob has three degrees from universities, my other brother Jock is an MA from Cambridge and I'm a BA from the Open University. As a player I was the one the manager would turn to last and say: "Right son, nothing clever from you this week."'

'You keep going because you love the game, the smell of the liniment, everything. I'm an adolescent about football. I'll quit when I grow up.'

SIR MATT BUSBY

Died: 1994 aged 84

'The greatest thing for a manager is to trust the talent.'

In 1956: 'Football has become a world game. It no longer belongs exclusively to England and Scotland. This is where the future lies.'

To his players: 'Don't be afraid to express yourselves.'

Crossing the bridge into Old Trafford for the first time after the 1958 Munich air disaster which claimed the lives of eight players and three club officials: 'I knew that the ghosts of the babes would still be there, and there they are still and will always be there as long as those who saw them still cross the bridge – young, gay, red ghosts.'

'All those lads you see going to the factories in Trafford Park, they have come to watch you on a Saturday. They have boring jobs, so you will have to give them something a bit special, something they will enjoy.'

'In all modesty, my summing up of the 1955–6 and

1956–7 seasons must be that no club in the country can live with Manchester United.'

'If you don't put them in then you can't know what you've got. If they are good enough, they are old enough.'

Asked if he thought Nobby Stiles was a dirty player: 'No, he's never hurt anyone. Mind you, he frightened a few!'

'It was a very simple team talk. All I used to say was, "Whenever possible, give the ball to George [Best]".'

On George Best: 'He was able to use either foot, sometimes he seemed to have six.'

'We had a few problems with the wee fella (Best) but I prefer to remember his genius.'

'Winning matches at all costs is not the test of true achievement; there is no dishonour in defeat as long as you play to the limit of your strength and skill. What matters above all things is that the game should be played in the right spirit, with fair play and no favour, with every man playing as a member of a team and the result accepted without bitterness and conceit.'

Ten years after Munich, United won the European Cup at Wembley: 'A dream fulfilled.'

'Played at its best between two first-class teams, football is a wonderful spectacle. I love its drama, its smooth playing skills, its carefully laid rhythms, and the added flavour of contrasting styles. Its great occasions are, for me at any rate, unequalled in the world of sport. I feel a sense of romance, wonder and mystery, a sense of beauty and a sense of poetry. On such occasions, the game has the timeless, magical qualities of legend.'

JACK CHARLTON

Born: 1935

'If Kevin Keegan fell into the Tyne he'd come up with a salmon in his mouth.'

'If in winning we only draw we would be fine.'

'I've seen them on TV on a Sunday morning most days of the week.'

'If I get a chance to do them I will. I will make them suffer before I pack this game in.

If I can kick them four years over the touchline I will.'

'It was a game we should have won. We lost it because we thought we were going to win it. But then again I thought there was no way we were going to get a result there.'

'We probably got on better with the likes of Holland, Belgium, Norway and Sweden, some of whom are not even European.'

'I won't die at a match. I might die being dragged down the River Tweed by a giant salmon, but a football match, no.'

'The honour that pleased me most of all was when the House of Commons voted me beer drinker of the year.'

After meeting the Pope in 1990: 'One of his cardinals introduced us, saying, "This is Mr Charlton." He said, "Ah yes, the boss!"'

BRIAN CLOUGH

Died: 2004 aged 69

'True fame is when the newspapers spell your name right in Karachi – and ordinary fame is when Mike Yarwood does you. Yarwood did me a favour. He made me popular. He advanced my cause.'

'I certainly wouldn't say I'm the best manager in the business – but I'm in the top one.'

To Derby players at a training session: 'Get in there – that's what I pay you for!'

To his Derby players, who were staying in the same Yugoslav hotel as some fans: 'These people have come two thousand miles to see you. Go and shake their hands and thank them.'

'People lose games. There is so much crap talked about tactics by people who barely know how to win at dominoes.'

'If we can stop hooliganism we can go a long way towards stemming the great tide of people not going to football matches.'

To Leeds players on his first day as manager: 'As far as I'm concerned you can throw all those medals you've won in the bin, because you won them all by cheating.'

Leaving Elland Road after being sacked just 44 days into his reign: 'This is a terrible day...for Leeds United.'

On his brief time at Leeds: 'I shouldn't have gone. I thought I could go there and win the European Cup. As things turned out, I'm not sure we ever won the toss!'

'They say Rome wasn't built in a day, but I wasn't on that particular job!'

'If a chairman sacks a manager that he initially appointed, then he should go as well.'

Referring to the long ball game: 'If God had intended us to play football in the clouds he would have put grass in the air.'

'Football is the most straightforward game on God's earth – beautiful grass, a ball, a defined space in which to play it.'

'It's easy enough to get to Ireland – just a walk across the Irish Sea as far as I'm concerned.'

'Most coaches overcomplicate football, as if it were something like nuclear physics and Einstein had written a book about it.'

'Why do so many people queue to see the Mona Lisa?

Because it moves them. They feel the same way about a beautiful woman, like Marilyn Monroe. They even feel the same way about a sunrise. Now if we're half as good-looking as a football team as Mona, Marilyn or a sunrise, then we might get one or two people prepared to come down and see us every Saturday – even if it's pissing down.'

On trying to achieve success with Brighton: 'It was like asking Lester Piggott to win the Derby on a Skegness donkey.'

After Brighton were beaten 4–0 in the FA Cup to part-timers Walton and Hersham: 'I lost to a team that sounded like a firm of solicitors.'

'I'd give anything for one more season as a player. If I could turn the clock back, that's what I'd do. You never lose the thrill of watching your own shot go past the goalkeeper.'

'I found that the only people who aren't obsessed with money are those who have got more than enough of it.'

'If a player had said to Bill Shankly, "I've got to speak to my agent," Bill would have hit him, and I would have held him while he hit him.'

Talking about Dutch football in 1985: 'Dutch goalkeepers

are protected to a ridiculous extent. The only time they are in danger of physical contact is when they go into a red light district.'

On why he was rejected by the FA for the England manager's job: 'They thought I was going to change it lock, stock and barrel. They were shrewd because that's exactly what I would have done!'

On England manager Bobby Robson: 'I'm fed up with him pointing to his grey hair and saying the England job has aged him ten years. If he doesn't like it, why doesn't he go back to his orchard in Suffolk?'

On his long-term coaching partner Peter Taylor: 'I'm the shop window – he's the goods at the back.'

On being linked with the Welsh manager's job in 1988: 'I can't promise to give the team talk in Welsh, but from now on I shall be taking my holidays in Porthcawl, and I've got a complete set of Harry Secombe records.'

On how to deal with a player disagreeing with his training methods: 'I'd ask him how he thinks it should be done, have a chat about it for about twenty minutes, and then decide I was right.'

On women's football: 'I like my women to be feminine and not rolling about in mud.'

On arriving at Nottingham Forest: 'I've left the human race and rejoined the rat race.'

'Our training ground was about as attractive as Siberia in midwinter without your coat on, and our training kit looked like something you got from an Oxfam shop.'

'Until we got hold of him, Kenny Burns couldn't crush a grape with a tackle. Now, Big Daddy would be frightened of going near him.'

Before Nottingham Forest's 1990 Littlewoods Cup Final: 'The only person certain of boarding the coach is Albert Kershaw – and he'll be driving it!'

In 1990: 'I hope you were as delighted as I was last week when Nelson Mandela was freed from a South African jail. But what I hadn't bargained for was that his release was going to cut across the start of our Littlewoods Cup Final.'

After receiving the freedom of Nottingham in 1993: 'It's a beautiful city with lovely people. The Trent is lovely too – I know, I've walked on it for years.'

'Outside of family life there is nothing better than winning European Cups.'

'My wife says OBE stands for Old Big 'Ead.'

After the FA had written to him complaining he had said he wanted to kick one of his own players: 'That bunch of shithouses at the Football Association – who know nowt – want to shut me up.'

After Alan Sugar's allegations about a 'bung' in 1995: 'The second he's brave enough, big enough, gets a bloody shave and doesn't walk like a spiv, then I'll sue him if he repeats it.'

'Football hooligans? Well, there are ninety-two club chairmen for a start.'

'Trevor Brooking floats like a butterfly and stings like one too.'

'Don't send me flowers when I'm dead, send them to me now if you like.'

On Sir Alex Ferguson's failure to match his record of two European Cups: 'For all his horses, knighthoods and championships, he hasn't got two of what I've got – and I don't mean balls!'

'If I wasn't getting the England manager's job in 1977, I was never getting it. All I had left was the European Cup. Winning it was my equivalent of the World Cup. Not many managers do *that* twice.'

At a press conference in Holland: 'Hey, Hitler only took

half an hour to get through this place – and he stopped for twenty minutes to make a cup of tea and to get a bite to eat on the way. The Dutch were waving him through – tanks this way, jeeps down that road.'

On Maradona's infamous 'hand of God' goal in the 1986 World Cup: 'Peter Shilton should have punched him.'

On the 1982 World Cup in Spain: 'If Taylor and I had got that job, we'd have won the bloody thing!'

'Resigning is for Prime Ministers and people caught with their pants down.'

'I only ever wanted to be manager of England. I'd have won the World Cup. Mind you, I'd probably have started a world war in the process.'

'I can tell, from the moment I see someone in the dressing room, whether he's off colour, had a row with his missus, kicked the cat or just doesn't fancy it that particular day.'

'If I find out that someone likes a bet, I can watch the size of his wallet. If I find out someone likes to chase women, I can see whether his fly is undone. If someone likes a beer, I'll get close enough to smell his breath in the morning. Now that's management.'

On Justin Fashanu, an openly gay player who wore

flamboyant clothes and expensive jewellery: 'If he wants to show off, why doesn't he just do it on the pitch?'

'It only takes a second to score a goal.'

'Do you know, Sinatra once met me.'

'Women run everything. The only thing I decided in my house over the last twenty years is to recognise Angola as an independent state.'

Talking about the offside law: 'If a player is not interfering with play, then he shouldn't be on the pitch.'

On wealthy footballers: 'I look at these talented and extremely fortunate young men and wonder whether, somewhere along the line, they were denied the chance to develop a proper sense of values. They can't know what money is worth because they have too much of it. You need to be a very level-headed young man indeed if you're to cope with millionaire status before the age of twenty.'

On Sven-Goran Eriksson's appointment as England manager: 'At last England have appointed a manager who speaks English better than the players.'

'I like the look of Mourinho. There's a bit of the young Clough about him. For a start he's good-looking.'

Asked what punishment he would have given to Eric Cantona for his kung fu attack on a Crystal Palace fan, he said: 'I would have cut off his testicles.'

After 17 years at Notts Forest: 'There was talk of a testimonial match, of a stand being named after me, but there was nothing, not even a toilet. They could have had a Brian Clough bog.'

'I know that most people will say that instead of walking on water I should have taken more of it with my drinks. They are absolutely right.'

After a transplant in 2003: 'To put everybody's mind at rest, I'd like to stress that they didn't give me George Best's old liver.'

'I never thought my body would reject my new liver. Reject – that's a word I've always hated since I was rejected for the England job.'

'When you get to a certain age, there is no coming back. I've decided to pick my moment to quit very carefully – in about two hundred years' time.'

'Who was that guy who said we'd all get fifteen minutes of fame? Andy Warhol wasn't it? Aye, well I've had a lot more than fifteen minutes' worth, so I can't complain.'

KENNY DALGLISH

Born: 1951

'If we score more goals than they do, we will win!'

'The Brazilians aren't as good as they used to be or as they are now.'

'It broke my heart to leave Liverpool.'

'As I've said before and I've said in the past...'

'What do I say to them in the dressing room? Nothing really. Most of the time I don't even know what they are going to do myself.'

'Management is a seven-day-a-week job. The intensity of it takes a toll on your health. Some people want to go on forever, and I obviously don't.'

'The people who come to watch us play, who love the team and regard it as part of their lives, would never appreciate Liverpool having a huge balance in the bank. They want every asset we possess to be wearing a red shirt.'

'Liverpool and Chelsea are close when they play each other, apart from the 4–1 at Anfield earlier this season, although they lost 2–0 down here.'

'At Liverpool we never accept second best.'

On John Barnes's Liverpool debut against Oxford in 1987: 'Barnes did what we expected him to do. He made a goal, scored one and entertained. You remember that.'

'The saddest and most beautiful sight I have ever seen.' Scarves and flowers at Anfield after the Hillsborough disaster.

'I owe Bob Paisley more than I owe anybody else in this game. There will never be another him.'

After veteran Ian Rush had joined John Barnes at Newcastle: 'We're developing our youth policy.'

On quitting Anfield in 1991: 'The pressure on match days is making my head explode. I can't go on.'

'I may have left Liverpool but the city and the club will always be part of me.'

TOMMY DOCHERTY

Born: 1928

'I talk a lot, on any subject. Which is always football.'

'Football management these days is like nuclear war – no winners, just survivors.'

'Players today are a pack of overpaid, pampered snot-nosed little ponces. Bring back national service for the lot of the bastards, I say.'

'Cricket is the only game where you can actually put on weight while you're playing.'

'On my first day as Scotland manager I had to call off practice after half an hour because nobody could get the ball off wee Jimmy Johnstone.'

On Doug Ellis, his chairman at Aston Villa: 'He said he was right behind me so I told him I'd rather have him in front of me where I could see him.'

On Mark Wright: 'He'd get an injury if he went on *Question of Sport.*'

'The ideal board of directors should be made up of three men, two dead and the other dying.'

'I've always said there's a place for the press, but they haven't dug it yet.'

'I don't think Henry Kissinger would have lasted forty-eight hours at Old Trafford.'

On Paul Gascoigne: 'He's a disgrace – thirty going on six.'

'If José Mourinho was made of chocolate he would lick himself.'

'This would cut hooliganism in half by 75 per cent.'

'Elton John decided he wanted to re-name Watford Queen of the South.'

'I hear Elton's made an offer for AC/DC Milan.'

'I'm sorry George Best couldn't be here tonight. He was launching a ship in Belfast but wouldn't let go of the bottle.'

'I've had more clubs than Jack Nicklaus.'

'My grasp of history is shaky to say the least but I don't

recall there being a winter break at the battle of the Somme.'

'Football wasn't meant to be run by two linesmen and air traffic control.'

'Tony Hateley had it all. The only thing he lacked was ability.'

In a 1963 match the winning goal came off the groin of a player called Harmer. Docherty said: 'In future Harmer should be known as the "cock of the north" or "the man with the secret weapon".'

'They serve a drink in Glasgow called a "Souness" – one half and you're off.'

On being sacked by Preston North End in 1981: 'They offered me a handshake of £10,000 to settle amicably. I told them they would have to be a lot more amicable than that.'

'Some teams are so negative they should be sponsored by Kodak.'

On Dwight Yorke after his Aston Villa debut in 1980: 'If that lad makes a first division footballer, then I'm Mao Tse Tung.'

'Robert Maxwell has just bought Brighton and Hove Albion, and he's furious to find out it's only one club!'

'I've been in more courts than Bjorn Borg.'

'Wimbledon have as much charm as a broken beer bottle.'

Docherty caused a scandal at Old Trafford when he ran off with the physiotherapist's wife Mary Brown, who he later married. He said: 'One of the United supporters came up to me and said if I could win the championship, he'd let me run off with *his* wife!'

SIR ALEX FERGUSON

Born: 1941

'When the wind's howling down the Clyde, that's what forges your character.'

'I was three years at the club [Dunfermline Athletic] and still hold the scoring record. That was in a Scottish first division where men were men, in the Kingdom of Fife!'

On his unsuccessful spell as a player for Rangers: 'No other experience in nearly forty years as a professional player and manager has created a scar comparable with that left by the treatment I received at Rangers.'

'Once I left Rangers, that was it. I don't look at Aberdeen's results either. The only team I look out for now is Benburb, my local junior team.'

'When I was at St Mirren it was a desolate place. Even the birds woke up coughing.'

On being fired by St Mirren: 'I learned a big lesson from

that part of my career ... because I didn't believe I could get the sack.'

Speaking about the Scotland job in 1980: 'Quite frankly I wouldn't take Jock Stein's job for a million pounds! Being manager of our national side is a thankless and difficult job... If I were in Jock's shoes then I would definitely go for a team comprising totally of home Scots.'

'When Paddy Crerand introduced me to Sir Matt (Busby) when I was still a player I was trembling, I was in awe. Those managers had control of their clubs and they had control of the press.'

'No manager is prepared for the job at Old Trafford...the legend is huge.'

'All this stuff about being a drinking club had to be addressed. I could never agree with those managers who think drinking is good for team spirit.'

'I have always considered that the player you produce is better than the one you buy.'

'Sometimes you have to be cold, clinical, and make judgements without compassion, even to a man you know like your own brother.'

'The lads ran their socks into the ground.'

'Cole should be scoring from those distances but I'm not going to single him out.'

'If we can play like that every week we'll get some level of consistency.'

'This pilot move by FIFA will take root and fly.'

'It's a conflict of parallels.'

'The philosophy of a lot of European teams, even in home matches, is not to give a goal away.'

'It was particularly pleasing that our goal-scorers scored tonight.'

'As with every young player, he's only 18.'

Alex Ferguson on Dennis Wise: 'He could start a row in an empty house.'

On Manchester United fans: 'We have people coming here to admire the scenery and enjoy their crisps.'

'Nicky Butt's a real Manchester boy, a bit of a scallywag. He comes from Gorton where it is said they take the pavements in of a night-time.'

'Of all the many qualities a good team must possess, the

supreme essential for me is penetration, and Eric (Cantona) brought the can-opener.'

In 1997, two years before he won the 'treble': 'Deep down, I know it would be impossible to win the League, the Champions Cup and the FA Cup.'

On winning the 'treble': 'I felt that if we could make it as champions then everything else would fall into place.'

At half-time during the 1999 European Cup final: 'At the end of this game, the European Cup will only be six feet away from you and you'll not even be able to touch it if we lose. And for many of you that will be the closest you will ever get. Don't you dare come back in here without giving your all.'

After the last-gasp victory over Bayern Munich to win the 1999 European Champions League final in Barcelona: 'I can't believe it. I can't believe it. Football – bloody hell!'

'It's been the greatest night of my life.'

'It would have been Sir Matt Busby's ninetieth birthday today, but I think he was up there doing a lot of kicking.'

'Just f***ing patch him up.' Ferguson to a club physio after kicking a boot at David Beckham's head which left him needing stitches above his eye.

On the same dressing room incident: 'It was a freakish incident. If I tried it a hundred or a million times it couldn't happen again.'

After reversing his 2000 decision to retire: 'I was worrying about what I was going to do at three o'clock on Saturday afternoons. I just couldn't see myself riding off into the sunset just yet.'

On the 2002–2003 end of season title race: 'It's getting tickly now – squeaky-bum time I call it.'

On the club's new 'Fortress Carrington' training ground: 'It keeps those f***ers from the media out.'

'I'm such a bloody talented guy. I might go into painting or something like that.'

On Paul Ince: 'He's a bully, a f***ing big-time Charlie.'

'I used to have a saying that when a player is at his peak, he feels as though he can climb Everest in his slippers. That's what he (Ince) was like.'

On Arsene Wenger: 'They say he's an intelligent man, right? Speaks five languages! I've got a fifteen-year-old boy from the Ivory Coast who speaks five languages!'

'David Beckham is Britain's finest striker of a football

not because of any God-given talent but because he practises with a relentless application that the vast majority of less gifted players wouldn't contemplate.'

'When an Italian tells me it's pasta on the plate I check under the sauce to make sure. They are the inventors of the smokescreen.'

Also on Italians: 'They come out with "The English are so strong, we're terrible in the air, we can't do this, we can't do that." Then they beat you 3–0.'

On Newcastle fans: 'They are so emotional and fanatical, they expect to win the World Cup!'

'Whether dribbling or sprinting, Ryan (Giggs) can leave the best defenders with twisted blood.'

Also on Giggs: 'I remember the first time I saw him. He was just thirteen and floated over the ground like a cocker spaniel chasing a piece of silver paper in the wind.'

'Pippo Inzaghi was born in an offside position.'

'If Chelsea drop points, the cat's out in the open. And you know what cats are like – sometimes they don't come home.'

On José Mourinho: 'He was certainly full of it, calling

me "boss" and "big man" when we had our post-match drink after the first leg. But it would help if his greetings were accompanied by a decent glass of wine. What he gave me was paint-stripper.'

'We will only be in trouble if we listen to José too much.'

'Wayne Rooney doesn't score tap-ins.'

'Wayne is truly blessed. He doesn't just have ability, he has a fire inside him.'

'When we signed him at eighteen, everyone said, "What will he be like at twenty-one?" Now he's twenty-one, people are saying, "What will he be like at twenty-five?" It was always destined to be that way.'

'When I was nineteen I was trying to start a workers' revolution in Glasgow. My mother thought I was a communist.'

On a row with goalkeeper Peter Schmeichel: 'He was towering over me and the other players were almost covering their eyes. I'm looking up and thinking, "If he does hit me I'm dead."'

On Ronaldo: 'I bet him he wouldn't get fifteen league goals and I'm going to have to change my bet with him. If he gets to fifteen I can change it and I'm allowed to do that because I'm the manager. I'm going to make it one hundred and fifty now!'

'What I tend to do is give myself other challenges. One was to learn the piano...it's good to have a challenge all the time to stretch yourself. I keep saying I'm going to go back to learning languages. I'm going to educate myself again.'

On owning racehorses: 'I've been a manager for twenty-eight years, having nothing else to focus on. It's a hectic job, and this has given me a release.'

On his postponed retirement: 'The critics were saying I'd lost my hunger and desire. You bet that hurt. I'd never had my desire questioned before. That's what really wound me up.'

'Management is all about control. Success gives you control and control gives you longevity as a manager.'

In January 2008 he said of Paul Scholes and Ryan Giggs: 'Bearing in mind their longevity, they must be the best two players I've ever had. I think I'll be away from the club before them!'

To tabloid reporters who suggested Juan Sebastian Veron had not been playing well: 'I'm not f***ing talking to you. He's a f***ing great player. Yous are f***ing idiots.'

On the proposal to play Premiership matches abroad: 'David Gill (United Chief Executive) told me to keep it quiet, and then it's all over the newspapers. Some people can't keep their mouths shut down there.'

When he was knighted at Buckingham Palace the Queen told him the 'treble' might never be achieved by an English club ever again. 'I have to agree with that,' replied Fergie.

On being made a freeman of Glasgow in 1999: 'Apparently I'm allowed to hang my washing on Glasgow Green, which is an interesting one. And if I ever get arrested in the city, I'm entitled to my own cell, which could come in handy at some point.'

'People say mine was a poor upbringing but I don't know what they mean. It was tough, but it wasn't bloody poor. We didn't have a TV. We didn't have a car. We didn't even have a phone. But I thought I had everything, and I did. I had a football.'

On Liverpool manager Rafael Benitez after his blistering verbal attack in 2009, claiming that Ferguson is never punished for criticising referees: 'There was a lot of venom in what he has said. He is obviously disturbed about something.'

SVEN-GORAN ERIKSSON

Born: 1948

On his £4 million annual salary for England: 'I have never understood it when people talk about my salary. There are others earning more than me, and why shouldn't an international manager be as well paid as a club manager?'

Before his first England game in 2001: 'I'm nervous about meeting so many people. It's like when you go out with a woman for the first time – you're bound to wonder how it will end up.'

After his first game: 'I feel I have broken the ice with the English people. In sixty days, I have gone from Volvo Man to Svensational.'

'I have never liked intrusion into my private life. But in the end you have to say "who cares?"'

On the 2006 World Cup in Germany: 'If we do not have too many injuries out in Germany, we will do a very good job. That is my conviction.'

'My dream is the same as your dream. The same as all the fans and players, that's to win a big tournament and win the World Cup.'

The day before England went out of the World Cup to Portugal in 2006: 'I won't read Winston Churchill the day before the game or try to be like him, though I did read some of his memoirs a long time ago. There are lots of leaders you have to admire – Bill Clinton, Tony Blair, who is very good at speeches, and Nelson Mandela – but I am not one of them.'

'David (Beckham) should think that talking is silver, but being quiet is golden.'

On Michael Owen: 'The thing about Michael is that he is fast, if defenders lose him for a moment they can't recover. Once Michael goes, they never catch him. On top of that is his finishing. He is so cold, even colder than a Swede.'

'I've always said that Crouch is special. He's tall and that makes him special. But he's special because he has good feet as well.'

After Wayne Rooney was sent off against Portugal in the 2006 World Cup: 'Don't kill him, I beg you, because you will need him. You can't take the temper out of Rooney.'

'I don't travel round the world with a school class. I'm not a school teacher or the father of a Sunday school.'

'The greatest barrier to success is the fear of failure.'

'If you want someone shouting, you will have to change the coach. I will never do it.'

'If you're the manager you're always responsible for the good times and the bad.'

'We need goals when the scoreline is 0–0.'

'Football is much harder if you don't have the ball.'

'I've read the book about all the other England managers. They were more or less killed, all of them. Why should I be different?'

At the height of speculation about an affair with Ulrika Jonsson: 'It's no good lying in your bed at night wondering if you have made the right choice.'

While at Manchester City in 2007: 'The English people are still very nice to me. They still want my autograph.'

'Don Revie was the cleverest of all of us England managers. He walked out before they threw him out.'

GEORGE GRAHAM

Born: 1944

'We're down to the bare knuckles.'

'The goalkeeper is the jewel in the crown, and getting at him should be almost impossible. It's the biggest sin in football to make him do any work.'

'The one thing I didn't expect is the way we didn't play.'

'There is only one person who knows how he ruined that sitter and that's Wayne Rooney, and even he doesn't know.'

'Wayne Rooney really has a man's body on a teenager's head.'

'The goal that Charlton scored has aroused Arsenal.'

'If Liverpool finish sixth and you get more points than them, you're looking at finishing fifth, or even fourth.'

'Nigel Winterburn was caught as immobile as a moving lamp-post.'

'They haven't lived up to the expectations we expect of them.'

On Thomas Brolin: 'I can't imagine him jumping for the ball. One of his false eyelashes might come out.'

'If footballers look after themselves there is no reason why they can't play until they are thirty-five – well maybe not you Quinny.' (Directed at Niall Quinn.)

'Playing another London side could be an omen, but I don't believe in omens.'

'I admit I'm single-minded. I think all of the great football managers have been single-minded.'

After being sacked by Arsenal in 1995 for taking a 'bung': 'The meeting with Rune Hauge (agent) was all very normal but the money came as a shock. I thought, "Jesus, what a Christmas present. Fantastic..." The ridiculous thing is it wouldn't have changed my life. I was on a good salary, but greed got the better of me. I'm as weak as the next man when it comes to temptation.'

'At least all the aggravation will keep me slim.'

'I will always have Arsenal-red blood running through my veins.'

RON GREENWOOD

Died: 2006 aged 84

'Playing with wingers is more effective against European sides like Brazil than English sides like Wales.'

'In comparison, there's no comparison.'

'Hoddle hasn't been the Hoddle we know. Neither has Robson.'

'I don't hold water with that theory.'

'I think everyone in the stadium went home happy, except all those people in Romania.'

'Being given chances, and not taking them. That's what life is all about.'

'To me personally, it's nothing personal to me.'

'Bryan Robson, well he does what he does and his future is in the future.'

'Bobby Moore was sent on this earth with ice in his veins.'

'They missed so many chances they must be wringing their heads in shame.'

RUUD GULLIT

Born: 1962

'When you're very young, you're the lovely little black boy with the curly hair. When you get older, it becomes an issue. I broke up a fight and the policeman saw my school books and said, "Ah, the nigger is studying, this nigger can count." My mother found this policeman and started swearing at him, and because she was white, he was really surprised and embarrassed.'

When named European Footballer of the Year in 1987, he dedicated his award to Nelson Mandela: 'I met Nelson Mandela after his release and he said, "Ruud, I have lots of friends now. When I was on the inside, you were one of the few."'

When a meeting with the great man was cancelled, Gullit said: 'I was just as disappointed as Mandela.'

Speaking in September 2007: 'Four months ago I visited Robben Island and met three guys who were cell-mates of Nelson Mandela. They remembered me dedicating my award in 1987 to Mandela and they said they couldn't believe what I had done, and were sure the football authorities would withdraw the award. That's what apartheid did to them, it made them believe injustice was a normal part of life.'

'Since Eriksson came to England, the guy who has been portrayed in the newspapers is not the guy I know. Sven is a gentleman, very likeable, very passionate and one who knows his football.'

'The great English strength is that they play with heart but that is not enough when they step out of the Premiership. Sometimes it is better to use your mind. I prefer to give 90 per cent sometimes and save 10 per cent with a little intelligence.'

'A team is like a clock. If you take one piece out, it doesn't work.'

'Football is part of life, but it is entertainment. There are other more important things.'

'A goalkeeper is a goalkeeper because he can't play football.'

'The more time you have, the more mistakes you will make.'

'To play Holland you have to play the Dutch.'

'We must have had 99 per cent of the game. It was the other 3 per cent that cost us the match.'

Announcing he will not go to the 1994 World Cup in the USA: 'I'm leaving now and I will never, never play for Holland again.'

Arriving at Chelsea in the summer of 1995: 'I drove until I got to Piccadilly Circus, taking in all the sights, and for the first time for a long, long time, I felt truly happy.'

Playing as a sweeper under Glenn Hoddle: 'I would take a difficult ball, control it, make space and play a good ball in front of the right back, except that he didn't want that pass. Eventually Glenn said to me, "Ruud, it would be better if you did these things in midfield."'

'Every time I played for Chelsea I thought, "nice game, beautiful stadium, great crowd, I'm playing well." It was the only time I really had fun.'

On his sacking from Chelsea in 1998: 'During my life, that had the biggest impact. As a human being, I had never been treated like that. I was shell-shocked for almost three months. I couldn't believe that people I worked with every day could do that. Bates sacked me, that was his right, but the information he based it on came from other people.'

'A Chelsea fan told me: "Ruud, you must never think bad of Chelsea. It was not Chelsea. It was just some people at Chelsea at that time." I was incredibly happy there. The memories are too good to be ruined by those who mistreated me.'

On his relationship with Alan Shearer at Newcastle: 'Everyone tried to leave Alan out of the team at times. Souness tried it, Bobby Robson tried it, they all tried, but Alan's bigger than the club.'

'I don't think we ever had a relationship. I felt he was a great player but that he could do better. He said to me, "I'm doing my best" and I knew exactly what he meant.'

On his bid to sign French winger Ibrahim Ba: 'You never sell the fur of a bear before you shoot it. I have brought my cannon with me.'

Commentating during Euro 96 in England: 'I am looking forward to seeing some sexy football tonight.'

In 2004 when he took over at Feyenoord: 'Sexy football is a phrase that has been totally taken out of perspective. I said it once, I think it was a game between the Czech Republic and Portugal. People repeat it to me wherever I go. They say there are some things you wish you never said in life – well that is mine!'

'It's the little things in football you miss. The smell of the grease and the oils, the tapping of the studs on the pavement, things like that.'

On his then partner Estelle, now his wife: 'It has become one big laugh between us, because she has told me, in all seriousness, "I thought you were a poof!" Can you imagine it – Rudi a poof!'

On his three wives and six children, two from each marriage: 'I have had a lot of personal troubles, but I ask myself, have I been so good at football because I have not been happy in my personal life? Football was my outlet. I could express myself in the best way. But I couldn't have both, a good private life and a good football career. The funny thing is that when I was in this situation, I thought, "I'm the only one. Typical black guy, goes there, makes mistakes." Then you look at people in normal life and all of a sudden you realise you're not the only one. Maybe the difference is that I can't hide it.'

GLENN HODDLE

Born: 1957

'I never heard a minute's silence like that.'

'Young David's young.'

'Seventy-five per cent of what happens to Paul Gascoigne is fiction.'

'His tackle was definitely pre-ordained.'

'I have a number of alternatives and each one gives me something different.'

'I think that the England job is tougher than being Prime Minister. The only time when things are more difficult for a Prime Minister is when he is making the decision to go to war and putting someone else's life on the line. The thing about being Prime Minister is that nobody really gets an opportunity to approach you and talk politics. But everywhere you go as England coach – if you are in a garage getting petrol, if you are in a restaurant having dinner with your wife, if you are in an airport lounge – you will have people telling you how to do your job.'

'Steven Carr has hit a small blimp.'

'I think in international football you have to be able to handle the ball.'

'Look at Jesus. He was a normal run of the mill sort of guy who had a genuine gift.'

'We threw caution to the wind and came back from the dead. Well, it is Easter Monday.'

'Robert Lee was able to do some running on his groin for the first time.'

'When a player gets to thirty, so does his body.'

'Okay, so we lost. But good things can come from it – negative and positive.'

'With hindsight, it's easy to look at it with hindsight.'

'He's a good footballer with a bit of everything and certainly two good feet, which is unusual these days.'

'Tuesday is very quick round the corner.'

'On reflection of this game it was probably an awkward time for us to score the third.'

'They were still in the dressing room when they came out for the second half.'

'If anyone is found guilty, I will step on them.'

'We didn't have the run of the mill.'

'International football is one clog further up the football ladder.'

'He was a player that hasn't had to use his legs even when he was nineteen years of age, because his first two yards were in his head.'

'Michael Owen is a goal-scorer – not a natural born one, not yet, that takes time.'

'That was the way to nail the record to the mast.'

'The FA Cup is still domestically the best cup in the world.'

'There was nothing wrong with the performance, apart from we threw away the game.'

'It's 60–40 against him being fit, so he's got half a chance.'

'You won't be surprised to know that I have some faith in astrologers and particularly what the stars predict for Scorpios.'

On the 1998 World Cup finals: 'At the end of the Argentina game I found myself asking the same question again and again: "Why am I here?"'

'My biggest mistake of the World Cup was not taking [faith healer] Eileen Drewery.'

Sadly for Hoddle he will always be remembered for this bizarre outburst in a 1999 interview, which cost him the England job: 'My beliefs have evolved in the last eight or nine years, that the spirit has to come back again. You have to come back to learn and face some of the things you have done, good and bad. You and I have been physically given two hands and two legs and half decent brains. Some people have not been born like that for a reason. The karma is working from another lifetime. It is not only people with disabilities. What you sow you reap.'

Later he claimed: 'At this moment in time I did not say them things.'

And in an interview in 2008 he said: 'I sometimes wonder about the fact that the FA set up the 1999 interview in the first place. One day I will put the record straight. One of my deepest regrets is that there are disabled people out there who still believe that I think those things.'

IAN HOLLOWAY

Born: 1963

'I am a football manager. I can't see into the future. Last year I thought I was going to Cornwall on my holidays but I ended up going to Lyme Regis.'

On what he described as an 'ugly' win against Chesterfield: 'To put it in gentlemen's terms, if you've been out for a night and you're looking for a young lady and you pull one, some weeks they're good-looking and some weeks they're not the best. Our performance today would have been not the best-looking bird but at least we got her in the taxi. She weren't the best-looking lady we ended up taking home, but she was very pleasant and very nice, so thanks very much, let's have coffee.'

'I reckon the ball was travelling at 400 miles per hour and I bet it burnt the keeper's eyebrows off.'

'It's like the film *Men in Black*. I walk around in a black suit, white shirt and black tie where I've had to flash my white light every now and again to erase some

memories, but I feel we've got hold of the galaxy now, it's in our hands.'

'When you're a manager it's a case of "have suitcase will travel", and I certainly don't want to travel with my trousers down.'

On QPR's potential: 'I call us the Orange club – because our future's bright.'

'It's all very well having a great pianist playing but it's no good if you haven't got anyone to get the piano on the stage in the first place, otherwise the pianist would be standing there with no bloody piano to play!'

On a linesman's performance: 'It was lucky that the linesman wasn't stood in front of me as I would have poked him with a stick to make sure he was awake.'

'Right now everything is going wrong for me – if I fell into a barrel of boobs I'd come out sucking my thumb.'

On veteran striker Paul Furlong: 'He is my vintage Rolls and he cost me nothing. We polish him, look after him and I have him fine tuned by my mechanics. We take good care of him because we have to drive him every day, not just save him for weddings.'

'I've got to get Dan Shittu ready for the Stoke game. I

told him to go to Iceland and ask if he can sit in one of their freezers.'

'You can say that strikers are very much like postmen, they have to get in and out as quickly as they can before the dog starts to have a go.'

'I've got to knock that horrible smell out of my boys because they smell of complacency.'

'Every dog has its day and today is woof day! I just want to bark!'

After a defeat by Notts County: 'We need a big, ugly defender. If we had one of them we'd have dealt with County's first goal by taking out the ball, the player and the first three rows of the seats in the stand.'

'There was a spell in the second half when I took my heart off my sleeve and put it in my mouth.'

After a ban on removing shirts to celebrate: 'I don't see the problem with footballers taking their shirts off after scoring a goal. They enjoy it and the young ladies enjoy it too. I suppose that's one of the main reasons women come to football games to see young men take their shirts off. Of course, they'd have to go and watch another game because my lads are as ugly as sin.'

After Manchester City's Joey Barton mooned at Everton

fans: 'It was a bit cheeky wasn't it? It would have been worse if he'd turned round and dropped the front of his shorts instead. I don't think there's anything wrong with a couple of butt cheeks personally. Maybe they're just jealous that he's got a real nice tight one, with no cellulite or anything.'

'I'm going to enjoy this win, take my brain out and stick it in an ice bucket.'

On Teddy Sheringham: 'He's the oldest swinger in town but at this level he will add a touch of class.'

On rumours of a knighthood for David Beckham: 'You're having a laugh. He's just a good footballer with a famous bird. Can you imagine if Posh was called Lady Beckham? We'd never hear the end of it.'

On his favourite TV show *The Dukes of Hazzard*: 'There was a woman who was quite well endowed and two boys who used to get drunk and have a fight – it had everything for me.'

On rumours in February 2008 that Leicester owner Milan Mandaric might sack him: 'Isn't it amazing? We lose a couple of games and everyone's got Milan swinging the axe. I suggest they come up with something cleverer than that. I've outlasted everyone else here this season so far!'

KEVIN KEEGAN

Born: 1951

'I'll never play at Wembley again, unless I play at Wembley again.'

'It's like a toaster, the ref's shirt pocket. Every time there's a tackle, up pops a yellow card. I'm talking metaphysically now of course.'

'The ref was vertically 15 yards away.'

'There are two schools of thought on the way the rest of this half is going to develop, everybody's got their own opinion.'

'Goalkeepers aren't born today until they're in their late twenties or thirties.'

'I don't think there is anyone bigger or smaller than Maradona.'

'England can end the Millennium as it started – as the greatest football nation in the world.'

'Even though two and two might look like four, it could be three or five.'

'That decision, for me, was almost certainly definitely wrong.'

'Sol Campbell using his strength there, and that is his strength. You could say that's his strong point.'

'One of his strengths is not heading.'

'Despite his white boots he had real pace.'

'He can't speak Turkish but you can tell he's delighted.'

'The ball was still moving when it hit the back of the net.'

'We deserved to win the game after hammering them 0–0 in the first half.'

'The good news for Nigeria is that they're 2–0 down very early in the match.'

'I risked getting my tyres nicked by going to Robbie Fowler's home in Liverpool.'

'There'll be no siestas in Madrid tonight.'

'My father was a miner, and he worked down a mine.'

'Gary Lineker always weighed up his options, especially when he had no choice.'

'I'm not disappointed, just disappointed.'

'Chile have three options – they could win or they could lose. The tide is in their court now.'

'Nicolas Anelka – twenty-four years of age but he has been around a lot longer than that.'

'Nicolas Anelka left Arsenal for £23 million and they built a training ground on him.'

'I came to Nantes two years ago and it's much the same today, except that it's completely different. The red light district is still the same, though it's a lot bigger and more expensive. I prefer Hamburg. There are these ladies there with fully formed moustaches.'

After signing Robert Lee from Charlton in 1994: 'He nearly went to Middlesbrough but I told him Newcastle was nearer London. Luckily footballers believe things like that.'

'That would have been a goal if it hadn't been saved.'

'People will say that was typical City, which really annoys me. But that's typical City I suppose.'

'They compare Steve McManaman to Steve Heighway, and he's nothing like him. But I can see why – it's because he's a bit different. They're both called Steve.'

'A tremendous strike which hit the defender full on the arm – and it nearly came off.'

'The only thing I fear is missing an open goal in front of the Kop. I would die if that were to happen. When they start singing "You'll Never Walk Alone" my eyes start to water. There have been times when I've actually been crying while I've been playing.'

'I know what is around the corner – I just don't know where the corner is. But the onus is on us to perform and we must control the bandwagon.'

'Hungary is very similar to Bulgaria. I know they're different countries.'

'In some ways, cramp is worse than having a broken leg.'

'Don't talk about the game, talk about Uriah Rennie [the ref] – that's what he likes and he's always been the same.'

'The thirty-three or thirty-four year-olds will be thirty-six or thirty-seven by the time the next World Cup comes around, if they're not careful.'

'England has the best fans in the world and Scotland's fans are second to none.'

'It is understandable that people are keeping one eye on the pot and another up the chimney.'

'Young Gareth Barry – he's young.'

'Argentina won't be at Euro 2000 because they are from South America.'

On Bill Shankly: 'I always carry a picture of him, he comes into my conversation a lot. I learned a lot from him and owe the man a great deal.'

'Everyone will remember his most famous comment – "Football's not a matter of life and death, it's much more important than that" – and he wasn't joking. He meant every word of it. He loved football and football people, but he wasn't keen on the periphery and the hangers-on.'

'Kanu, a guy with a heart as big as he is.'

'Football's always easier when you've got the ball.'

Preparing to become England manager: 'The day I don't get emotional about football, I'll be back playing golf again in Spain.'

'I want more from David Beckham, I want him to improve on perfection.'

'There's a slight doubt about only one player, and that's Tony Adams, who definitely won't be playing tomorrow.'

After quitting as England manager in 2000: 'I have no complaints. Absolutely no one is to blame but myself. I did the job to the best of my ability. I am not the man to take it that stage further. I have to be true to myself. Kevin Keegan has given it his best shot. I told the players I don't think I can find that little bit extra you need at this level.'

'The last thing I want is to be known as the man who lost the last game at Wembley.'

'Some parts of the job I did very well, but not the key part of getting players to win football matches.'

'The Germans only have one player under twenty-two, and he's twenty-three.'

'We managed to wrong a few rights.'

'The substitute is about to come on. He's the player who was left out of the starting line-up today.'

'He's about as tall as they get for a goalkeeper of six-foot-five.'

'If I had a blank piece of paper, there would be five names on it.'

'A lot of my time is taken up thinking adventurously.'

'I can take the pressure of the clock ticking on the wall.'

'I'd love to be a mole on the wall in the Liverpool dressing room at half-time.'

'I've had an interest in racing all my life, or longer really.'

'Romeo Benetti. I was at a social function with him the other week and it's the first time I've got within ten yards of him that he hasn't kicked me. Even then I kept looking over my shoulder.'

'Batistuta is very good at pulling off defenders.'

'Luis Figo is totally different to David Beckham and vice versa.'

To ITV viewers just before Dan Petrescu scored for Romania in the 1998 World Cup: 'Only one team can win this now – England.'

After Portugal beat England at Euro 2000: 'Portugal play football as I like to see it played. As a neutral it was fantastic. Unfortunately I'm not a neutral.'

After Newcastle lost to Manchester United in 1995: 'The circus came to town but the lions and tigers didn't turn up.'

On the crowd at Newcastle's St James's Park: 'You can't force people to sit down even if they have a seat. They want to sing and, unless you're Val Doonican, you can't do that sitting down.'

'You get bunches of players like you do bananas, though that is a bad comparison.'

During his first press conference at Manchester City: 'My mum always told me not to go near the main road.'

After branding referee Steve Dunn a 'homer' following Newcastle's 4–3 win over his Manchester City side in 2004: 'That was wrong and I owe him a letter of apology for that.'

His infamous rant against Alex Ferguson during the 1995–96 season, when Newcastle lost a 12-point lead – and the Premiership – to Manchester United and Ferguson claimed that teams tried harder against United than Newcastle: 'He's gone down in my estimation. We're still fighting for this title and I'll tell you honestly I would love it if we beat them – LOVE IT!'

'I haven't watched a game of football since my last match at Manchester City. And I cannot even remember what that game was.'

After leaving Manchester City: 'Football today is not my type of football.'

Back at Newcastle in 2008: 'When they've worked hard all week they come here to be entertained. It's like people down south going to the theatre. They want to enjoy it. What they don't want is for us to go out, play drably, win 1–0 and maybe finish halfway up the table. They want us to have a go – that's why I'm here.'

On learning that his first transfer target, Jonathan Woodgate, had signed for Spurs: 'They are in Europe this year. I can't offer that unless we get on a ferry.'

On the proposal to play some Premiership games abroad: 'It will be pretty tough for Geordies working nine to five during the week to get to Dubai, Beijing or Auckland. But sometimes it's worth trying new things.'

In September 2008, after only eight months in charge, Keegan left Newcastle for a second time. He said: 'It's my opinion that a manager must have the right to manage and that clubs should not impose upon any manager any player that he does not want.'

HOWARD KENDALL

Born: 1946

'You can have love affairs with other football clubs. With Everton it's a marriage.'

On Peter Reid joining QPR: 'Peter's legs looked all right. But the hooped shirt didn't do him any favours!'

Before an FA Cup tie at Stoke City in 1984 he threw open the dressing room windows to let the players hear the roar of 10,000 Everton fans. 'That's your team talk – don't let them down.' Everton won 2–0.

'I have the honour of being the most successful manager in the history of Everton football club, one of the greatest and biggest clubs in the world.'

Encouraging Chelsea to play well against Bolton: 'Hopefully they won't be wearing their flip-flops as they have been in the last couple of games.'

Replying to a jibe from Brian Clough that he was simply a 'young pup': 'I'm a hush puppy now.'

After a sending off: 'I don't think that the contact was as severe as the player made out. That part of the pitch was uneven, but it won't need rolling now.'

'My autobiography, which was written by Ian Ross.'

STEVE McCLAREN

Born: 1961

After Middlesbrough were beaten 7–0 by Arsenal: 'Every defeat hurts. You might think it doesn't, but you ask my family, you ask the dog.'

'If we want to improve on last season then this is a side we have to beat.'

'Rochemback has got their certain something we've been missing, the X-faction in the midfield department.'

'Everybody has their opinion and likes to state it, and if that's what he wants to say then that's what he wants to say.'

'We learned a lot last season about three games a week.'

'I don't sell porn. I don't sell lottery tickets. I don't sell cigarettes or low-end screw tops.'

'We're delighted with just the 1–0. I thought the first half was very good but in the second half we made mistakes. It could have been worse, 2–0 or 3–0.'

'I'm fighting hard, it's difficult under the weight of criticism but you have to take it.'

'I do not read the papers, I don't gamble, I don't even know what day it is.'

'We conceded two quick goals over there and we're capable of doing the same at home.'

After a poor performance against Andorra in March 2007 he stormed out of a press conference saying: 'Gentlemen, if you want to write whatever you want to write, you can write it, because that's all I am going to say.'

'This is getting totally out of hand.'

JOSE MOURINHO

Born: 1963

Introducing himself to the English press in 2004: 'Please don't call me arrogant, but I'm European champion and I think I'm a special one.'

'If I wanted to have an easy job...I would have stayed at Porto – beautiful blue chair, the UEFA Champions League trophy, God and after God, me.'

After Porto's 2003 UEFA Cup Final victory over Celtic: 'There was a lot of commitment in Celtic's game, commitment, toughness and aggression. I'm tempted to use another word – but I won't.'

After his Porto team beat Manchester United in 2004: 'I understand why Sir Alex Ferguson was a bit emotional. You would be if your team got clearly dominated by one built on ten per cent of your budget.'

'People think the reason I went to Chelsea was financial. I'm not a hypocrite – I don't say that the money isn't important for my family. But the reason I went there was to work under pressure.'

On his predecessor at Chelsea, Claudio Ranieri: 'I could say, "What has he ever won?" but I won't.'

'For me, pressure is bird flu. I'm feeling a lot of pressure with the problem in Scotland. It's not fun and I'm more scared of it than football.'

'Look at my haircut. I am ready for the war.'

'I did it [had my hair cut] because I want to push my son to do the same. I also did it because I want to push the young players on my team to have a proper haircut, not the Rastafarian or the others they have.'

'The moral of the story is not to listen to those who tell you not to play the violin but to play the tambourine.'

On his famous training manual: 'Respect for the club, for its norms, for its philosophy etc, is much more important than any other individual. The document I drew up, and which some now refer to as the bible, is totally in line with this principle.'

On a Chelsea injury crisis: 'It's like having a blanket that is too small for the bed. You pull the blanket up to keep your chest warm and your feet stick out. I cannot buy a bigger blanket because the supermarket is closed. But the blanket is made of cashmere!'

'Young players are a little like melons. Only when you

open and taste the melon are you 100 per cent sure that the melon is good.'

'Sometimes you see beautiful people with no brains. Sometimes you have ugly people who are intelligent, like scientists. Our pitch is a bit like that. From the top it's a disgrace but the ball rolls at normal speed.'

'We all want to play great music all the time, but if that's not possible, you have to hit as many right notes as you can.'

Reporter: 'Do you believe in God?'
Mourinho: 'I think more important is love. Love is what matters.'

On Petr Cech's serious head injury: 'A player from Man City showed half of his ass for two seconds and it was a big nightmare. But this is a real nightmare.'

After a Sheffield United fan threw a bottle at Frank Lampard: 'Maybe the guy drank red wine or beer with breakfast instead of milk.'

'My wife is the real manager of family life. You are the star outside, here you are not a star.'

'I've only been to a pub once and that was to get cigarettes for my wife at 11.30 in the evening. I prefer bars to sit and drink tea or coffee.'

Waiting to hear if he will be allowed to watch Arsenal versus Manchester United: 'It all depends on my wife. If I am at home, yes, I will see it. But maybe my wife would like to go somewhere. I would like to see it – I like to see football and it is a big game. But maybe I will have no permission.'

After the fracas over his Yorkshire Terrier: 'My wife is in Portugal with the dog. The dog is with my wife so the City of London is safe, the big threat is away.'

On William Gallas missing a pre-season match in the USA: 'As you know, Gallas had an unbelievable holiday. I hope he enjoyed it very much in Guadeloupe, which I think is a fantastic place to be on holiday, so he wanted to stay there for a long time.'

'If you ask me if I jump with happiness when I know Mr Poll is our referee? No.'

'Wenger has a real problem with us and I think he is what you call in England a voyeur. He is someone who likes to watch other people. There are some guys who, when they are at home, have this big telescope to look into the homes of other people and see what is happening. Wenger must be one of them – and it is a sickness.'

Still on Wenger: 'Many great managers have never won the Champions League – a big example is not far from us.'

On Liverpool's Rafa Benitez: 'Three years without a Premiership title? I don't think I would still be in a job.'

'Liverpool are favourites because in the year 2007 we've played twenty-seven matches and Liverpool play three or four.'

After losing to Liverpool in the Champions League semi-final: 'The best team lost.'

On Barcelona's Lionel Messi: 'How do you say "cheating" in Catalan? Barcelona is a cultural city with many great theatres and this boy has learned very well. He's learned play acting.'

On Blackburn's watered pitch: 'During the afternoon it rained only in this stadium – our kitman saw it – they tried everything. There must be a microclimate here. The pitch was like a swimming pool.'

'Places like Bramall Lane are the soul of English football. The crowd is magnificent, saying "F*** off Mourinho" and so on.'

'We have eight matches and eight victories, with sixteen goals, but people say we cannot play, that we are a group of clowns. This is not right.'

After a roller-coaster 3–2 win over Birmingham: 'Entertaining? Too much!'

On Arsenal 5, Spurs 4 in November 2004: 'That was not a football score, it was a hockey score. In training I often play matches of three against three and when the score reaches 5–4 I send the players back to the dressing room, because they are not defending properly.'

'If I don't go to the semi-final then I will go to the wrestling at Earl's Court with my kids.'

Just before leaving Chelsea: 'The style of how we play is very important. But it is omelettes and eggs. No eggs – no omelettes! It depends on the quality of the eggs. In the supermarket you have class one, two or class three eggs and some are more expensive than others and some give you better omelettes. So when the class one eggs are in Waitrose and you cannot go there, you have a problem.'

'After fifteen years, I'm an overnight success!'

'It was a beautiful and rich period of my career. I want to thank all Chelsea supporters for what I believe is a never-ending love story.'

In February 2009, while manager at Inter Milan, Mourinho hinted his heart was still with Chelsea: 'If you are asking me if you think one day I will return to Chelsea, I tell you, "Yes, I think so," although I'm not saying when. We were so happy together.'

BILL NICHOLSON

Died: 2004 aged 85

'If you don't drag yourself off the pitch exhausted after ninety minutes, you can't claim to have done your best.'

'Intelligence doesn't make you a good footballer. Oxford and Cambridge would have the best sides if that were true. It's a football brain that matters and that doesn't usually go with an academic brain. In fact I prefer it when it doesn't. I prefer players not to be too good or clever at other things. It means they concentrate on football.'

'If you don't win anything, you have had a bad season.'

'When it is played at its best, football remains the greatest game of all.'

'The public can't be kidded. They know what they want to see, what is good and what is bad, and what is just average. At least I believe they do.'

'It's been my life, Tottenham Hotspur, and I love the club.'

'There's no use being satisfied when things are done wrongly. I want perfection.'

'It is better to fail aiming high than to succeed aiming low. And we at Spurs have set our sights very high, so high in fact that even failure will have in it an echo of glory.'

'It's magnificent to be in Europe – if we're not in Europe, we're nothing. We're nothing.'

MARTIN O'NEILL

Born: 1952

After becoming Celtic manager in 2000, on the prospect of abuse from Rangers fans: 'I am not even liked in my own household, so I'll be fine.'

On declining to become a Celtic director: 'Managing the football team is hard enough without going on the board and deciding whether to sack myself or not.'

'I will calm down when I retire or die.'

'My ban might be good news for the players. The last thing they want to see is a nervous wreck of a manager who's speaking nonsense.'

'If the players are looking for a sign from me, I'm sorry but I'll be in the toilet somewhere. It's not my job to keep everyone happy. I'm not a social worker.'

'I'd dearly love to have played lead guitar with Jethro Tull. That would have done me. I saw Tull playing Birmingham Odeon in 1974 and they had a fellow called Jeffrey Hammond-Hammond who made Pete Townshend look ninety.'

On his unsuccessful bid to become England manager in 2006: 'If Brian Clough, who had an ego the size of fifteen houses, had the humility to go for an interview for the job, the rest of us mortals should be able to subject ourselves to that.'

Asked if Aston Villa could win the Premiership in 2009: 'Don't be silly.'

BOB PAISLEY

Died: 1996 aged 77

'Mind you, I've been here during the bad times too. One year we came second!'

'I remember Jimmy Adamson crowing after Burnley had beaten us that his players were in a different league. At the end of the season they were.'

'The sort of lad I'm looking for here is a kid who'll try to nutmeg Kevin Keegan in a training match, but then step aside for him in the corridor.'

Talking about Alan Kennedy's debut as a Liverpool player: 'I tell you something, they shot the wrong Kennedy.'

'One of the things I keep reminding players is that when you're lost in a fog, you must stick together. Then you don't get lost. If there's a secret about Liverpool, that's it.'

After winning the 1977 European Cup in Rome against Borussia Moenchengladbach: 'You won't find anyone sober in Rome tonight, apart from me, the Pope and

Horace Yates [a staunch teetotal sportswriter]. This is the second time I've beaten the Germans here. The first was in 1944. I drove into Rome on a tank when the city was liberated.'

On Billy Liddell: 'Bill was so strong it was unbelievable. You couldn't shake him off. It didn't matter where he was playing, though I suppose his best position was outside left. He could go round you, past you or straight through you sometimes.'

'I just hoped that after the trials and tribulations of my early years in management, someone up high would smile on me and guide my hand. My plea was answered when he got me Kenny Dalglish. What a player, what a great professional.'

'Sponsors! They'll be wanting to pick the team next.'

DAVID PLEAT

Born: 1945

'That would have put the icing on his start.'

'For such a small man, Maradona gets great elevation on his balls.'

'I was inbred into the game by my father.'

'Our central defenders, Doherty and Anthony Gardner were fantastic, and I told them when they go to bed tonight they should think of each other.'

'Apart from John Terry, Chelsea are a team of immigrants. Where's Veron now? Where's Petit? And where's that full-back from Holland, what's his name, Bogarde? Is he still making films? I feel sorry for Ranieri because he is something of a gipsy and Chelsea have kept him out of the picture.'

'And the steam has gone completely out of the Spanish sails.'

'I've seen some players with very big feet and some with very small feet.'

'There's Thierry Henry, exploding like the French train that he is.'

'Winning isn't the end of the world.'

'He's got a brain under his hair.'

'We just ran out of legs.'

'Pires has got something about him, he can go both ways depending on who's facing him.'

To a seventeen-year-old Neil Ruddock: 'When you finish playing football young man, which I feel will be very soon, you will make a very good security guard.'

'If there are any managers out there with a bottomless pit, I'm sure they would be interested in these two Russians.'

'Stoichkov is pointing at the bench with his eyes.'

'He hits it into the corner of the net straight as a nut.'

'The man we want has to fit a certain profile. Is he a top coach? Would the players respect him? Is he a nutcase?'

'We came here with a game plan but parked it at the gate.'

'We like a tackle at Tottenham. We're not pansies you know.'

SIR ALF RAMSEY

Died: 1999 aged 79

After his Ipswich team won the league in 1962: 'I feel like jumping over the moon.'

In 1963 after being named England manager: 'England will win the World Cup in 1966.'

'Never change a winning team.'

After England beat Argentina 1–0 in the 1966 quarter-final at Wembley, when their captain Antonio Rattin was sent off: 'It seemed a pity so much Argentinian talent is wasted. Our best football will come against the right type of opposition – a team who come to play football, and not act as animals.'

After beating Portugal in the semi-finals, he told the players in a hotel bar: 'Gentlemen, congratulations on a fine performance and on making the final. Tonight you may have two pints – and I mean two pints. Not like last Saturday night after the Argentina game when, how shall I put it, some of you were rat-arsed.

But not tonight gentlemen. Just two pints. Because on Saturday you are going to win the World Cup, and when you do I shall see to it that you are permanently pissed.'

To Nobby Stiles on the eve of the final: 'Are you ready for tomorrow? You bloody well better be.'

His famous pep talk before extra time in the 1966 World Cup final: 'You've won it once. Now you'll have to go out there and win it again.'

In 1967: 'I am not one to jump over the moon or off a cliff.'

'When England win, everything belongs, quite rightly, to the players. They are the people who have made victory possible. When England loses, it is my responsibility. But football management is a double-edged thing. On one hand the manager gets too much credit, on the other, he takes too much of the blame. I have never looked for praise. It makes me uncomfortable.'

'There is great harmonium in the dressing room.'

'Bobby Moore could play in his overcoat and not break in to a sweat.'

'Pelé has nearly everything. Maradona has everything.'

104

He once told a group of Scottish players: 'Now I know you lot f***ing hate me. Well I have news for you. I f***ing hate you lot even more.'

Reporter: 'Welcome to Scotland.'

Ramsey: 'You must be f***ing joking.'

After being knighted in 1967: 'I shall clobber the first player who calls me Sir Alfred. I accepted this honour because the fact that somebody else in the game is now a "Sir" [Stanley Matthews was honoured in 1965] should lift the whole of football a little bit.'

After Alan Mullery was sent off for kicking a Yugoslavian player in the groin who had been fouling him throughout the game, Alf told him: 'If you hadn't done I would have!'

'A footballer's wife needs to run the home completely so that he has no worries; give him the sort of food he likes and should have; and to work only for his good and the good of his career. She must know that she will rarely see him at weekends, and the better player he is, the less she will see of him. A footballer could be ruined by a wife who let him have all the household responsi- bilities, fed him the wrong diet and gave him no peace of mind. My wife has been splendid. I have been very lucky.'

On Brian Clough after the Derby manager withdrew Roy McFarland on the eve of a crucial England match in April 1972, claiming he was injured: 'The man calls himself a patriot, but he has never done anything to help England. All he does is criticise us in the newspapers and television.'

In 1973 England drew with Poland at Wembley and failed to qualify for the 1974 World Cup finals in Germany: 'If Bobby Moore had wept, we would have all wept with him,' said Sir Alf, who then lost his job.

'If we had beaten Poland 10–1 it would have been a fair reflection of the play. The fact that we only drew 1–1 was beyond belief. I saw Ipswich chairman John Cobbold after the match and he described it as more one-sided than Custer's last stand.'

'It was the most devastating half-hour of my life,' he later said of his sacking. 'I stood in a room almost full of staring committee men. It was just like I was on trial. I thought I was going to be hanged.'

CLAUDIO RANIERI

Born: 1951

As he joined Chelsea in 2000: 'I am a lovely man as long as everyone does what I say.'

'Driving a car in England is still a problem. If I am alone on the road I begin to ask whether I am driving on the right side. And when I go back to Italy I have started to wonder the same thing. It is confusing.'

'My team showed good stamina and good vitamins.'

'I was like Pavarotti out there, trying to stimulate my players.'

'My team is like an orchestra. To play the symphony correctly I need some of the boom-boom but also some of the tweet-tweet. Sometimes the boom and the tweet go well together.'

'The team is my baby. When it is ready to get out of the pram, I will lead it by the hand.'

'I am happy when our fans are happy, when our players are happy and our chairman is on the moon.'

'This is my culture. I am Italian. In Italy, you win one match, draw the second and are sacked by the third.'

'I saw the "Save Ranieri" campaign in the *Evening Standard* with a little picture of me. It was very flattering except for one thing: if I'm to fight like a gladiator, they can't run a picture of me wearing my glasses. Gladiators don't wear glasses in the Colosseum.'

'The Manchester City challenge reminds me of my experience at Chelsea, where we built a good team without spending £1. I created the Chelsea miracle from nothing and my achievement convinced Roman (Abramovich) to buy the club.'

HARRY REDKNAPP

Born: 1947

'Hartson's got more previous than Jack the Ripper.'

'Lomana LuaLua probably doesn't even know what a 4–4–2 is but when we switched to it he stuck to his position out wide and did a great job.'

On keeping Southampton in the Premiership: 'It's like being on the *Titanic* and seeing there is only one lifeboat left, and we are all trying to dive into it!'

Asked if he had ever received any death threats: 'Only from the wife when I didn't do the washing up.'

'I don't know this guy Velimir Zajec and I will never know him and he will never know me. Never. No chance. It won't happen.'

'With the foreign players it's more difficult. Most of them don't even bother with the golf, they don't want to go racing. They don't even drink.'

'I stood there all day with a plastic angel in my pocket. I believe in fate – I'm as silly as a bunch of lights.'

While West Ham manager in 2000: 'I told my chairman that David O'Leary spent £18 million to buy Rio

Ferdinand from us and Leeds have given O'Leary £5 million in share options, whereas I bring in £18 million and all I get is a bacon sandwich.'

On going back to Portsmouth as manager again: 'If I said I'd go back now I'd be crucified – that's all I need!'

'We went to watch a show, Billy Joel. Half of the foreign lads weren't quite sure who Billy Joel was, but I enjoyed it. For the Charlton game I'll really punish them – I'll take them to see *Mamma Mia*.'

On Jermain Defoe: 'He's cocky and arrogant, but show him a goal and he's away like a wind-up toy.'

'After shooting practice yesterday I had to drive up the M27 and collect four balls.'

'Smassi Aboa don't speak the English too good.'

'I don't like silly phone-in programmes. People come on who don't know what the hell they are talking about and say things like "sack the manager because the team played crap today".'

'Dani is so good-looking I don't know whether to play him or f*** him.'

'Even when they had Moore, Hurst and Peters, West

Ham's average finish was about seventeenth. It just shows how crap the other eight of us were.'

'Where are we in relation to Europe? Not far from Dover.'

'I tape over most of the player videos with *Corrie* or *Neighbours*. Most of them are crap. They can f***ing make anyone look good. I signed Marco Boogers on the evidence of a video sequence of his best moments. He was a good player but a nutter. They didn't show that on the video.'

'Van Persie obviously thought, "Why take the piss out of poor old Southampton? I'll get sent off and make a game of it."'

On Sir Alex Ferguson, the man he calls the Godfather of Football: 'I'm not going to say this is my last contract. When I finish this one, I'll still be two years younger than Sir Alex is now, and I'll still look younger.'

On Iain Dowie: 'By the look of him he must have headed a lot of balls.'

'I sorted out the team formation last night lying in bed with the wife. When your husband's as ugly as me, you'd only want to talk about football in bed.'

'Mansfield gave us [Portsmouth] one hell of a game. I

feared extra time but we are still on the march, still unbeaten, and I'm still a brilliant manager.'

'The Del Boy comparisons piss me off. I'm not like him at all. I've been married thirty-five years and this is my third football club in twenty-odd years. I'm not a ducker and diver.

I may be a Cockney, but that doesn't mean I fit some silly stereotype.'

'I'll be mightily relieved when this transfer window closes. Morning, noon and night over the past few weeks it has been non-stop phone calls. I took the missus out for a meal. I was outside the restaurant for a good hour and a half negotiating with three other parties.'

'I don't get involved in transfers in any way, shape or form.'

DON REVIE

Died: 1989 aged 61

'I've been in the game too long to start slagging off the referee. But I'll be very surprised if he's got a father to confess to.'

Trying to gee up a lazy player: 'I'm going to get the cheque book out!'

To his squad: 'Keep your hair short, your clothes smart and don't get caught up with loose girls.'

Revie hated FA boss Sir Harold Thompson, who told him at a dinner: 'When I get to know you better, Revie, I shall call you Don.' Revie replied: 'When I get to know you better, Thompson, I shall call you Sir Harold.'

'I think that winning a trophy is almost the easiest part of the exercise. Retaining it, and at the same time, one's sense of purpose, modesty and place in things, is infinitely more difficult.'

Telling how he got the England job: 'I made the first

move. They did not contact me. I fancied being England manager.'

After leaving England in 1977: 'As soon as it dawned on me that we were short of players who combined skill and commitment, I should have forgotten all about trying to play more controlled, attractive football and settled for a real bastard of a team.'

After 32 Leeds fans were arrested following a pitch invasion: 'I don't blame them at all. The referee's decision in allowing West Bromwich Albion's second goal was diabolical.'

On Eddie Gray: 'When he plays on snow he doesn't leave any footprints.'

SIR BOBBY ROBSON

Died: 2009 aged 76

'Titus looks like Tyson when he strips off in the dressing room, except he doesn't bite and he has a great tackle.'

'What can I say about Peter Shilton? Peter Shilton is Peter Shilton and has been Peter Shilton since the year dot.'

On why he would not name his England team too early before a World Cup qualifier against Sweden in 1989: 'Hitler didn't tell us when he was going to send over the Doodlebugs, did he?'

'I would have given a right arm to have been a pianist.'

On life in Barcelona: 'Look at those olive trees. They're two hundred years old – long before the time of Christ.'

'I'm not going to look beyond the semi-final, but I would love to lead Newcastle out at the final.'

'In a year's time, he's a year older.'

'His influence on the team through his personality and playing ability cannot be underestimated.'

'In all my time as a player I never won a thing.'

'Anything from 1–0 to 2–0 would be a nice result.'

'The margin is very marginal.'

'We've got nothing to lose, and there's no point in losing this game.'

'He's got his legs back, of course, or his leg – he's always had one but now he's got two.'

'I thought individually and as a pair, they'd do better together.'

'We just haven't had the rub of the dice.'

'We mustn't be despondent. We don't have to play them every week, although we do play them next week as it happens.'

'I've only got two words for how we played out there tonight – not good enough.'

'That little lad Paul Parker has jumped like a salmon and tackled like a ferret.'

'Until we're out of the Champions League, we're still in it.'

'Jermaine Jenas is a fit lad. He gets from box to box in all of ninety minutes.'

After Millwall fans rioted against Ipswich: 'They should have turned flame throwers on them.'

'Where do you get an experienced player like him with a left foot and a head?'

'Sarajevo isn't Hawaii.'

'If you are a painter you don't get rich until after you are dead. The same happens with managers. You're never appreciated until you've gone and all the people say: "Oh he was okay, just like Picasso."'

On Paul Gascoigne: 'Daft as a brush.'

Also on Gazza: 'When he was dribbling he used to go through a minefield with his arm, a bit like you go through a supermarket.'

'For a player to ask for a transfer has opened everybody's eyebrows.'

'Denis Law once kicked me at Wembley in front of the

Queen at an international. I mean, no man is entitled to do that really.'

'He's not the Carl Cort that we know he is.'

'Gary Speed has never played better, never looked fitter, never been older.'

'The first ninety minutes are the most important.'

'Home advantage gives you an advantage.'

'Eighteen months ago Sweden were arguably one of the best three teams in Europe, and that would include Germany, Holland, Russia and anybody else if you like.'

'Well, we got nine and you can't score any more than that.'

'I do want to play the short ball, and I do want to play the long ball...I think long and short balls is what football is all about.'

'He's very fast and if he gets a yard ahead of himself nobody will catch him.'

'My father had five sons and I have four brothers.'

'If we start counting our chickens before they hatch, they can't lay any eggs in the basket.'

At PSV Eindhoven in Holland: 'An English pro accepts the manager's decisions.'

'After every match here the substitutes come and visit me.'

'They are two points behind, so we are neck and neck.'

'I played cricket for my local village. It was forty overs per side and the team that had the most runs won. It was that sort of football.'

'Both teams, and Brazil even, got better on their way to the World Cup Final.'

'We don't want our players to be monks. We want them to be football players because a monk doesn't play football at their level.'

'All right, Bellamy came on at Liverpool and did well, but everyone thinks he's the saviour, he's Jesus Christ. He's not Jesus Christ.'

'We didn't underestimate them, they were just a lot better than we thought.'

'Practice makes permanent.'

'Robert said I was picking the wrong team, and I was because he was in it.'

'We've introduced some movement into Shearer's game now. Last season he played with one leg, this season he's got two.'

'Tottenham have impressed me. They haven't thrown in the towel even though they've been under the gun.'

'Players never know why they're taken off or substituted until they become managers.'

On José Mourinho: 'Two things struck me straight away. The standard of José's English and the fact that he was a nice-looking boy. Too good-looking for my liking.'

After Shay Given was nutmegged twice by Marcus Bent of Ipswich Town: 'I'm looking for a goalkeeper with three legs.'

'Some of the goals were good, some of the goals were sceptical.'

'They can't change any of their players, but they have changed one of their players and that's the coach.'

'Their football was exceptionally good – and they played some good football.'

'I'd say he's the best in Europe, if you put me on the fence.'

'There will be a game where somebody scores more than Brazil, and that might be the game that they lose.'

On Maradona's infamous 'hand of God' goal in the 1986 World Cup against England: 'It wasn't the hand of God. It was the hand of a rascal. God had nothing to do with it. That day Maradona was diminished in my eyes forever.'

On calls for his resignation after England's failure at the Euros in 1988: 'If the pressure had frightened me, I'd have kept my quality of life at Ipswich. I'd have kept driving my Jag six miles to work every day and got drunk with the chairman every Saturday night.'

'We've got great speed in the team, not just Gary Speed, but great speed.'

'I said to the lads in the dressing room at half-time, I said there was nothing to say.'

On England's semi-final defeat against Germany in the 1990 World Cup: 'Not a day goes by when I don't think about the semi-final and other choices I might have made.'

On emerging from a lift he said to Bryan Robson: 'Hello Bobby.'

The England captain replied: 'No boss, me Bryan, *you* Bobby!'

'We're flying on Concorde, it'll shorten the distance, that's self-explanatory.'

On his first day at Newcastle: 'On my way here I followed a car with the number plate SOS1. Perhaps someone was trying to tell me something.'

'I intend to be at St James's Park as long as my brain, heart and legs all work...simultaneously.'

'I bleed black and white.'

On the delights of Tyneside: 'If we invite any player up to the Quayside to see the girls, and then to our magnificent stadium, we will be able to persuade any player to sign.'

On learning Shakira was staying at the same Barcelona hotel as his players: 'We used to have Shaka Hislop on our books but I've never heard of Shakira – is she a singer?'

'Everyone's got tough games coming up. Manchester United have got Arsenal, Arsenal have got Manchester United, and Leeds have got Leeds.'

At Newcastle in 2003: 'We're in a dogfight and the fight

in the dog will get us out of trouble. We are solid behind each other, and through being solid we will get out of trouble and, if that fails, then we will be in trouble, but that's not the situation here. We'll all get in the same rowing boat, and we'll all pick up an oar and we'll row the boat.'

After being made an Honorary Freeman of the city of Newcastle: 'The proudest moment of my life.'

'Football is my life, my obsession, my hobby, my theatre.'

As he left the England job: 'I'm here to say goodbye – maybe not goodbye, but farewell...'

JOE ROYLE

Born: 1949

'I don't make promises. I promise results.'

'We played well for the first ninety minutes.'

After Oldham had been knocked out of the FA Cup by Spurs in 1988: 'Ossie Ardiles was the difference – it was like trying to tackle dust.'

'Life at Oldham is like being a nitroglycerine juggler.'

'Of their goals, two came from headers, and one was a header.'

'I can't take responsibility for the referee handing out bookings if people breathe too heavily.'

'I don't blame individuals, I blame myself.'

'That was clearly a tackle aimed at getting revenge – or maybe it was just out-and-out retribution.'

In 1994 while Everton manager: 'We don't have reporters any more; we have QCs. Nowadays they aren't interested in how many goals a player scores, but where he's scoring at night.'

'Duncan Ferguson became a legend before he became a player.'

'I've seen players sent off for worse than that.'

'The Italians can blame no one but themselves. They can blame the referee, but they can blame no one but themselves.'

'If it had gone in, it would have been a goal.'

'There are no easy games in this division, and this one won't be easy.'

After Manchester City's September 1998 visit to Millwall: 'I can't believe what I've seen tonight. It was a disgrace. If we'd scored another goal in that atmosphere I don't think we would have got out alive.'

'I may be a Scouser but I'm not stupid.'

'I might have been the captain when we went down, but not when we hit the iceberg.'

LUIZ FELIPE SCOLARI

Born: 1948

In 1999, while at Brazilian club Palmeiras: 'If someone talks about my private life, I'll give them a good punching. I'm not interested in suing. I like to sort things out my way.'

'General Pinochet tortured a lot of people, but there is no illiteracy in Chile.'

On his conditions for joining Barcelona before taking charge of Brazil in 2001: 'I wouldn't accept fifty trucks of cash if they didn't let me appoint my own coaching staff.'

'I will go down as the Brazil coach that lost to Honduras.'

'I'm going home to give my wife a big hug, because I doubt if I can manage anything else.'

'I don't express very well and some newspapers write different to what I think.'

While at Chelsea: 'You know how many people live in

Brazil? One hundred and eighty million and I was there. You think here is pressure? It is zero pressure. Pressure was when I was coach of the national team because everyone in Brazil is the coach.'

After being sacked from Chelsea: 'At Chelsea we don't have a player who can make the difference by himself and do something magical on the pitch.'

BILL SHANKLY

Died: 1981 aged 68.

'Someone said, "Football's a matter of life and death to you," and I said, "Listen, it's more important than that."'

'There's only two teams in Liverpool – Liverpool and Liverpool reserves.'

'Ladies and gentlemen, today we are joined by a man who ranks amongst the greatest there is. Shakespeare, Rembrandt and Bach. This man is Dixie Dean.'

Then at Dixie Dean's funeral: 'I know this is a sad occasion but I think that Dixie would be amazed to know that even in death he could draw a bigger crowd than Everton can on a Saturday afternoon.'

'I don't think I was in a bath until I was fifteen years old. I used to use a tub to wash myself. But out of poverty, with a lot of people living in the same house, you get humour.'

'My idea was to build Liverpool into a bastion of invincibility. Napoleon had that idea. He wanted to conquer

the bloody world. I wanted Liverpool to be untouchable. My idea was to build Liverpool up and up until eventually everyone would have to submit and give in.'

'My life is my work. My work is my life.'

To a trainee player: 'The trouble with you, son, is that all your brains are in your head.'

After beating Everton in the 1971 FA Cup semi-final: 'Sickness would not have kept me away from this one. If I'd been dead, I would have had them bring the casket to the ground, prop it up in the stands and cut a hole in the lid.'

'I was the best manager in Britain because I was never devious or cheated anyone. I'd break my wife's legs if I played against her, but I'd never cheat her.'

'At a football club there's a holy trinity – the players, the manager and the supporters. Directors don't come into it. They are only there to sign the cheques.'

'I'm just one of those people who stands on the Kop. They think the same as I do, and I think the same as they do. It's a kind of marriage of people who like each other.'

To Ian St John: 'If you're not sure what to do with the

ball, just pop it in the net and we'll discuss your options afterwards.'

On Tommy Smith: 'If he isn't named footballer of the year, football should be stopped and the men who picked any other player should be sent to the Kremlin.'

'Football is a simple game based on the giving and taking of passes, of controlling the ball and of making yourself available to receive a pass. It is terribly simple.'

After Alan Ball had signed for Everton: 'Don't worry Alan, at least you'll be able to play close to a great team!'

'He has football in his blood,' a scout told Shankly, who replied: 'You may be right, but it hasn't reached his legs yet!'

To a fan: 'Where are you from?'

Fan: 'I'm a Liverpool fan from London.'

Shanks: 'Well, laddie, what's it like to be in heaven?'

'When the ball's down the Kop end, they frighten the ball. Sometimes they suck it into the back of the net.'

To the players after failing to sign Lou Macari in 1973: 'I only wanted him for the reserves.'

Tommy Docherty: 'You have to say Tony Hateley's good in the air.'

Shanks: 'Aye, so was Douglas Bader ... and he had a wooden leg.'

Discussing a player with Tommy Docherty:

Doc: '100,000 wouldn't buy him.'

Shanks: 'Yeah, and I am one of the 100,000.'

To a Brussels hotel clerk who queried 'Anfield' as his address: 'But that's where I live!'

To Kevin Keegan: 'Just go out and drop a few hand grenades all over the place son.'

To Tommy Smith after he'd turned up for training with a bandaged knee: 'Take that poof bandage off, and what do you mean you've hurt your knee? It's Liverpool's knee!'

To Peter Thompson as he struggled to reproduce the form he had shown in an England game against Brazil: 'The white Pelé? You're more like the white Nellie!'

Sportswriter to Shanks: 'I think Tony Currie's display was reminiscent of Tom Finney, Bill.'

Shanks: 'You could be right. Mind you, Tom's fifty-seven.'

To Celtic manager Jock Stein after a Euro tie at Anfield: 'Jock, do you want your share of the gate money or shall we just return the empties?'

After a 5–1 defeat by Ajax in the 1967 European Cup: 'We cannae play these defensive continental sides.'

On a wartime England v Scotland match: 'We absolutely annihilated England. It was a massacre. We beat them 5–4.'

'Roger Hunt misses a few, but he gets in the right place to miss them.'

'If you are first you are first. If you are second you are nothing.'

'I don't drop players, I make changes.'

'I'm a people's man, a player's man. You could call me a humanist.'

'The trouble with referees is that they know the rules, but they do not know the game.'

'Anything off the top?' asked his barber in 1968. 'Aye, Everton,' replied Shankly.

To an interpreter translating for excited Italian journalists:

'Just tell them I completely disagree with everything they say.'

After a hard fought 1–1 draw: 'The best side drew.'

'It's a ninety minute game for sure. In fact I used to train for a one hundred and ninety minute game so that when the whistle blew at the end of the match, I could have played for another ninety minutes.'

To hard man Tommy Smith: 'You, son, could start a riot in a graveyard.'

'I told this player, "Listen, son, you haven't broken your leg, it's all in the mind."'

'Sorry boss, I should have kept my legs together,' said keeper Tommy Lawrence after letting in a fluke goal.

'No, Tommy, your mother should have kept her legs together!' replied Shanks.

'If Everton were playing at the bottom of the garden, I'd pull the curtains.'

'Of course I didn't take my wife to see Rochdale as an anniversary present – it was her birthday. Anyway it was Rochdale reserves.'

To new signing Ian St John: 'Son, you'll do well here as long as you remember two things. Don't over-eat and don't lose your accent.'

After signing Ron Yeats: 'With him in defence we could play Arthur Askey in goal.'

'Although I'm a Scot I'd be proud to be called a Scouser.'

On Brian Clough: 'He's worse than the rain in Manchester. At least God stops the rain in Manchester occasionally.'

But when a photographer suggested Clough was too outspoken, Shankly told him: 'Laddie, that man scored two hundred goals in two hundred and seventy matches – an incredible record – and he has won cup after cup as a manager. When he talks, pin back your ears.'

'It's great grass at Anfield, professional grass.'

'A football team is like a piano. You need eight men to carry it and three who can play the damn thing.'

On his resignation: 'It was the most difficult thing in the world. When I went to tell the chairman, it was like walking to the electric chair, that's the way it felt.'

'I've been so wedded to Liverpool that I've taken Nessie

(his wife) out only twice in forty years. It's time she saw more of my old ugly mug.'

On retirement: 'I have not been short of invitations to other clubs and have been received more warmly by Everton than I have by Liverpool. It's probably fair to say that they are now "my" team.'

'The socialism I believe in is everybody working for the same goal and everybody having a share in the rewards. That's how I see football, that's how I see life.'

During a lap of honour in April 1973 a fan threw his scarf at Shankly and it was flung to one side by a policeman. Shankly picked up the scarf and reprimanded the policeman, telling him: 'Don't do that. This might be someone's life.'

JOHN 'JOCK' STEIN

Died: 1985 aged 62

'We must play as if there are no more games, no more tomorrows.'

To his players before the 1967 European Cup Final: 'Coming here you've made history. Go out and play to your capabilities, and enjoy yourself!'

On winning the trophy: 'We did it by playing football, pure inventive football.'

'After all we're a small country [Scotland]. The Finns and the Norwegians, you don't get them saying, "We're going to win the World Cup."'

'We do have the greatest fans in the world, but I've never seen a fan score a goal.'

'Celtic jerseys are not for second best. They don't shrink to fit inferior players.'

On Bill Shankly: 'I don't believe everything Bill tells me about his players. Had they been that good they would not only have won the European Cup, but the Ryder Cup, the Boat Race and even the Grand National.'

'Football is nothing without the fans.'

On England captain Bobby Moore: 'There should be a law against him. He knows what's happening twenty minutes before everyone else.'

'We all end up as yesterday's men in this business. You're quickly forgotten.'

'The best place to defend is in the opposition's penalty box.'

'There is no substitute for experience.'

GORDON STRACHAN

Born: 1957

'If a Frenchman goes on about fishing boats and sardines, he's called a philosopher. I'd just be called a short Scottish bum talking crap.'

'I've got more important things to think about, I've got a yoghurt to finish by today. The expiry date is today.'

'I used to drive home from Manchester United's training ground along the M56 and there was a left turn for Wilmslow, where I lived, and a right turn for Hale, where Norman Whiteside, Paul McGrath and Bryan Robson lived. I used to say that it was left for under three pints a night and right for more than ten!'

To a reporter who said, 'You don't take losing lightly, do you Gordon?'
'I don't take stupid questions lightly either.'

On Wayne Rooney's fame: 'It's an incredible rise to stardom. At seventeen, you're more likely to get a call from Michael Jackson than Sven-Goran Eriksson.'

To a reporter who asked for a 'quick word': 'Velocity!' said Strachan, marching off.

After a superb performance from striker James Beattie: 'I would like to thank James's parents for what they did twenty-five years ago.'

To a bunch of sports writers: 'You people are sometimes like those serial killers you see in films who leave out the words like "I'm going to get you" or "your wife is next".'

'The world looks a totally different place after two wins. I can even enjoy watching *Blind Date* and laugh at *Noel's House Party*.'

On being assaulted in 1980: 'It's always great being attacked. He got fined £100 for that but they had a whip round in the pub and he got £200.'

On Alex McLeish: 'We even competed for the acne cream when we were younger – obviously I won that one!'

On Claus Lundekvam after he was carried off at Leicester: 'Someone asked me if he was unconscious, but I didn't have a clue. He's always like that.'

Reporter: 'Welcome to Southampton. Do you think you are the right man for the job?'

Strachan: 'No. I was asked if I thought I was the right man for the job and I said, "No, I think they should have got George Graham because I am useless."'

Reporter: 'So, Gordon, in what areas do you think Middlesbrough were better than you today?'
Strachan: 'What areas? Mainly that big green one out there.'

'The ref said, "If I make a mistake don't make me look an idiot." I had a great idea lined up but it would have cost me a couple of quid.'

'I've had better weeks. I tried to make it better by playing my dad at golf on Sunday. We played thirteen holes and I got beat by a sixty-year-old man with a bad limp.'

'We're fourth in the table! Just hope nobody gets nosebleeds. I'm going home and I'm going to sit with a bottle of Coke, a packet of crisps and stare at the Teletext league tables for three hours.'

On heat treatment and ice packs: 'My bum has been through every temperature known to man.'

'If there was a Champions League for guts and determination we would be in with a chance of winning it.'

On Sir Alex Ferguson: 'He used to play tapes of Bill

Shankly talking. I remember that, and a singer he liked. I don't know who it was but he was crap. He played it on the team bus too and all the boys hated it, until one night it got chucked away. If he's still wondering who threw that tape off the bus, it was me. So maybe he's right and I'm not to be trusted.'

To Bolton player Jardel: 'When you go and speak to your mates and they ask what you contributed to the game, you say: "I fell, I fell like a big Jessie!"'

'I know how people see me, but all my life I've been a victim of self-doubt. There have been many times when I have felt despondent, when I think I'm useless. I felt it many times as a player and I've often experienced it as a manager.'

'When I'm dead it will be inscribed on my tombstone: "This isn't as bad as that night in Bratislava."'

After clinching the title with Celtic in 2007: 'I've never taken drugs but I wonder if it's a bit like this.'

'We owe the English big time. They stole our land, our oil, perpetrated the Highland Clearances and now they've even pinched Billy Connolly.'

GRAHAM TAYLOR

Born: 1944

'To be really happy, we must throw our hearts over the bar and hope that our bodies will follow.'

'Shearer could be at 100 per cent fitness, but not peak fitness.'

'It's the only way we can lose, irrespective of the result.'

'The effort I think you should take for granted, but sometimes it's not there.'

'Nothing that UEFA or FIFA do surprises me anymore and I'm very surprised this has not been sorted out long in advance.'

'People always remember the second half.'

'In football, time and space are the same thing.'

'Very few of us have any idea whatsoever of what life is

like living in a goldfish bowl – except of course for those of us who are goldfish.'

'It's a game we've got to win. It's also a game we've not got to lose.'

'I'd never allow myself to let myself call myself a coward.'

'In 1972 I was one of twenty-four players at Lincoln City. The manager was sacked and seven days later I was the manager of twenty-three players.'

'Being a manager can be a very lonely job. You've got to believe in yourself. We didn't win a game in my first eleven matches at Lincoln. I well remember the call of three thousand people: "Taylor out, Taylor out!" '

A fan of ballet and theatre, Taylor says: 'What I think the dancer has over and above the footballer is a dedication to practice.'

'I haven't seen a dancer disagree with the instructor and tell him he doesn't know what he's talking about – you can see that on a football pitch.'

'Dancers earn in a year what a so-so Premiership player earns in a week. Now I think footballers could learn something from that.'

'If he opens his legs he'll be hard to handle.'

On his relationship with Aston Villa chairman 'Deadly' Doug Ellis: 'Well, it's a love–hate relationship and he loves me.'

'Sometimes it's very hard to follow what would have happened and sometimes it's hard to follow what has happened.'

Before a 0–0 draw with Denmark in Euro 92: 'I expect to win, let me do the worrying, that's what I get paid for. You get your feet up in front of the telly, get a few beers in and have a good time.'

'What a clinical finish. That's got nothing to do with his haircut at all – that's footballing ability.'

'The thing about coming to watch football in this part of the world is it makes you realise what a world game it is.'

'There may have been a problem with the wall of two or two and a half players.'

'He knows they've got to score three goals. They know they've got to score three goals. What more can you say?'

'That's a goal isn't it, but what a good save!'

'I think what would help the Ecuadorian side is if they could get a glimpse of the possibility of scoring a goal.'

As England failed to qualify for the 1994 World Cup in the USA, the unfolding disaster was captured on a fly-on-the-wall Channel 4 documentary, *An Impossible Job*. It produced Taylor's most famous quote, 'Do I not like that!' as a back pass was intercepted and England conceded a goal against Poland. The programme was re-named and released on video.

After a 2–0 defeat to Norway in a 1993 World Cup qualifier: 'We made a complete mess of it. I'm here to be shot at and take the rap. I have no defence.'

'I sometimes wished I'd been shot. Though it never came to that – nor should it.'

Chasing a linesman down the Rotterdam touchline after the referee failed to send off Ronald Koeman of Holland for upending David Platt as he looked certain to score: 'Hey! Hey! Tell your pal that he's just cost me my job. Thank him very much for that, will you?'

'Can we not knock it? They've done everything that we told them not to do.'

'It was nearly my finest hour, but life is made up of so-nearlies.'

'Napoleon wanted his generals to be lucky. I don't think he would have wanted me.'

TERRY VENABLES

Born: 1943

'You either win or you lose. There's no in between.'

'If you can't stand the heat in the dressing room, get out of the kitchen. The mere fact that he's injured stops him getting injured again, if you know what I mean.'

'People say I should concentrate on being a football person, but what does that mean? Get home in the afternoon and go to the betting shop, the pub and the snooker hall? All I've done is try to learn how to use a typewriter. Sorry about that!'

'If history is going to repeat itself I should think we can expect the same thing again.'

At Barcelona in 1984: 'When I arrived in the summer, one of my predecessors told the Spanish press that 'Meester' Terry would be gone by Christmas, but he forgot to say which year.'

'The main thing I miss about London? The sausages.'

'A lot of people seem to think I'm just a slippery Cockney boy with a few jokes. It's taken one of the biggest clubs in the world to acknowledge what I can really do – coach.'

After a bad run which led to his sacking from Barcelona: 'I can still go out as long as it's after midnight, I'm wearing dark glasses and it's a dimly lit restaurant.'

On Terry Fenwick's drink-driving charge: 'The spirit he has shown has been second to none.'

'There are two ways of getting the ball. One is from your own team-mates, and that's the only way.'

'It's understandable and I understand that.'

'Certain people are for me, certain people are pro me.'

'If you can't outplay the opposition, you must outnumber them.'

'I felt a lump in my mouth as the ball went in.'

On controversy over his business dealings in 1994: 'I must be the only person who actually gets less publicity by becoming manager of England.'

'Everybody says Steve McManaman played on the left

for me in Euro 96 but he never played on the left. The one time he did play on the left was against Switzerland.'

'I've been asked that question for the last six months. It's not fair to expect me to make such a fast decision on something that has been put upon me like that.'

Jimmy Hill: 'Don't sit on the fence, Terry. What chance do you think Germany has of going through?' Venables: 'I think it's fifty-fifty.'

'He's got a great future ahead. He's missed so much of it.'

'I had mixed feelings – like watching my mother-in-law drive over a cliff in my car.'

'It was never part of our plans not to play well, it just happened that way.'

'Apart from their goals, Norway haven't scored.'

'It may have been going wide, but nevertheless it was a great shot on target.'

'They didn't change positions. They just moved their players around.'

'Those are the sort of doors that get opened if you don't close them.'

On making the most of life: 'There's plenty of time to rest when you're dead.'

ARSENE WENGER

Born: 1949

'You have to be a masochist to be an international manager.'

On Sir Alex Ferguson: 'His weakness is that he doesn't think he has any.'
Also: 'When we meet in airports we don't fight. These meetings are even funny.'
And: 'I am ready to take the blame for all the problems of English football if that's what he wants.'

On the proposal to play some Premiership games abroad: 'If money is the first priority then forget it, because it will become a circus. It would be nice to play in China because there are two billion people there – let's take the whole league there?'

'What is remarkable is that Thierry Henry does not have the game of a goal scorer.'

On star striker Thierry Henry staying at Arsenal for the money: 'I didn't think it's because of my eyes, my beautiful eyes!'

And when Henry left for Barcelona: 'It was Thierry's decision to leave Arsenal, but he goes with my blessing.'

Accusing Spurs manager Martin Jol: 'Do you really believe he didn't see anything? He was right in front of him.

He says he didn't see it but frankly I don't believe him – he is lying!'

'I don't kick dressing room doors, or the cat, or even journalists.'

'I like to read a book or talk to my wife or daughter, for an hour or so. But to have a whole day without thinking about football – that is impossible.'

'You live in a marginal world as a manager. I know three places in London: my house, Highbury and the training ground.'

On Owuse-Abeyie: 'I wish I could use 'Quincy' on his shirt, but they won't let us. I don't know how to pronounce his name, I've tried but I can't.'

On transfer approaches: 'If people come to your window and talk to your wife every night, you can't accept it without asking what is happening.'

'One of the difficulties of our job is that we create eleven unemployed people when you name the squad, and then on Monday we employ them again as if nothing has happened.'

'It was a very bad night. We were very disappointed with the quality of our performance. I could cry – maybe it would be easier – but life goes on.'

After Arsenal fielded no England players against Crystal Palace in 2005: 'England boss Sven was here – so who did he watch then? Has he signed for a different country?'

'You cannot say you are happy when you don't win.'

Wenger's reply to Patrick Vieira, who complained that Arsenal had failed to sign any world-class players: 'You weren't a world-class player when Arsenal signed you!'

On signing José Reyes: 'We didn't think he would play on Sunday because he was suspended. That makes me think he has all the qualities to join Arsenal.'

'The issue of nationality is irrelevant. Whenever you represent a club it's about value and qualities, not about passports.'

'Maybe it's my birthday, I'm fifty-eight. There's not much I need. I have plenty of socks.'

'I place huge importance on the opinions of the fans. Supporters are the democratic voice of the club. Their opinion of the manager evolves in the same way as political opinion polls. Things fluctuate but there is a consistent core.'

'Of the nine red cards this season we probably deserved half of them.'

'He made the impossible possible.'

'Davor has a left leg and a nose in the box.'

'As long as no one scored, it was always going to be close.'

'I didn't see it.'

MISCELLANEOUS MANAGERS

Some managers don't deserve a section of their own...but these one-liners are too good to leave out!

Partick Thistle manager **John Lambie**, when told a concussed player did not know who he was: 'That's great, tell him he's Pelé and get him back on.'

Terry Neill: 'I'm not superstitious or anything like that, but I'll just hope we play our best and put it in the lap of the gods.'

Gareth Southgate: 'I remember before we beat Chelsea a couple of years ago, I said that if we could put a man on the moon, we can beat Chelsea. If you believe they put a man on the moon, then anything is possible.'

Watford's **Adrian Boothroyd** on Marlon King and Darius Henderson: 'There are times when they look telepathic and there are times when they look as if they haven't met each other.'

Howard Wilkinson after signing Eric Cantona for Leeds:

'Eric gave interviews on art, philosophy and politics. A natural room-mate for David Batty, I thought immediately.'

Berti Vogts: 'If I walked on water, my accusers would say it is because I can't swim.'

Walter Smith: 'If we'd won, it would have meant an historic double-treble. But we weren't even thinking about that.'

Keith Hill (Rochdale): 'You can compare us at the moment to a bit of soft porn. There is an awful lot of foreplay and not a lot going on in the box.'

Kevin Bond (Bournemouth): 'I enjoy being a manager – except for Saturday afternoons.'

Peter Reid: 'In football, if you stand still, you go backwards.'

Bruce Rioch: 'We threw our dice into the ring and turned up trumps.'

Graeme Souness: 'The referee has a reputation for trying to make a name for himself.'

Bobby Gould: 'Give him his head and he'll take it with both hands or feet.'

Bryan Robson: 'We're going to start the game at nil-nil and go out and try to get some goals.'

Dave Bassett: 'And I honestly believe we can go all the way to Wembley – unless somebody knocks us out.'

Gerry Francis: 'What I said to them at half-time would be unprintable on the radio.'

Andy Roxburgh: 'Hagi is a brilliant player, but we're not going to get psychedelic over him.'

Lawrie McMenemy: 'When you are 4–0 up you should never lose 7–1.'

Gianluca Vialli: 'At the start of the season you're strong enough to win the Premiership and the European Cup, but you have to be as strong in March, when the fish are down.'

Alex Smith: 'We had enough chances to win this game. In fact we did win.'

Mick McCarthy: 'I was feeling as sick as the proverbial donkey.'

John Toshack: 'Winning all the time is not necessarily good for the team.'

Graham Rix: 'Their keeper played very well and it was not the best pitch, but I'm not making excuses.'

Giovanni Trappatoni: 'We can't behave like crocodiles and cry over spilled milk and broken eggs.'

Don Howe: 'At the end of the day, the Arsenal fans demand that we put eleven players on the field.'

Carlton Palmer: 'I said to the players before the start, "Just go out and give it 100 per cent." I'm not asking for any more than that.'

Dave Jones: 'Overall I think we dominated for 75 per cent of the game, but we do have to make sure we do that for the other 15.'

Howard Wilkinson: 'We have to roll up our sleeves and get our knees dirty.'

Gerard Houllier: 'You can't say my team aren't winners. They've proved that by finishing fourth, third and second in the last three years.'

Neil Warnock: 'Matches don't come any bigger than FA Cup quarter-finals.'

Chelsea's **Dave Webb**: 'Compared to the chairman I had at Southend, Ken Bates is Mary Poppins.'

Johan Cruyff: 'I don't believe in God. In Spain all twenty-two players cross themselves. If it works, the game is always going to be a draw.'

Dave Bassett: 'When I arrived here the board said there would be no money – and they have kept their promise.'

Stuart Pearce: 'I can see a carrot at the end of the rainbow.'

Gerry Francis: 'The day I got married, Teddy Sheringham asked for a transfer. I spent my honeymoon in a hotel room with a fax machine trying to sign a replacement.'

Dave Sexton: 'The way forwards is backwards.'

Mike Walker: 'I just wonder what would have happened if the shirt had been on the other foot.'

Terry Butcher: 'The beauty of cup football is that Jack always has a chance of beating Goliath.'

Sam Allardyce: 'Our major problem is that we don't know how to play football.'

In 2009 Liverpool boss **Rafael Benitez** launched an extraordinary attack on Sir Alex Ferguson: 'He was not punished. He is the only manager in the league that cannot be punished for these things.' [Verbally attacking referees.]